THE IMPACT OF GOVERNMENT
ON REAL ESTATE FINANCE
IN THE UNITED STATES

Relation of the Directors to the Work and Publications
of the National Bureau of Economic Research

1. The object of the National Bureau of Economic Research is to ascertain and to present to the public important economic facts and their interpretation in a scientific and impartial manner. The Board of Directors is charged with the responsibility of ensuring that the work of the National Bureau is carried on in strict conformity with this object.

2. To this end the Board of Directors shall appoint one or more Directors of Research.

3. The Director or Directors of Research shall submit to the members of the Board, or to its Executive Committee, for their formal adoption, all specific proposals concerning researches to be instituted.

4. No report shall be published until the Director or Directors of Research shall have submitted to the Board a summary drawing attention to the character of the data and their utilization in the report, the nature and treatment of the problems involved, the main conclusions and such other information as in their opinion would serve to determine the suitability of the report for publication in accordance with the principles of the National Bureau.

5. A copy of any manuscript proposed for publication shall also be submitted to each member of the Board. For each manuscript to be so submitted a special committee shall be appointed by the President, or at his designation by the Executive Director, consisting of three Directors selected as nearly as may be one from each general division of the Board. The names of the special manuscript committee shall be stated to each Director when the summary and report described in paragraph (4) are sent to him. It shall be the duty of each member of the committee to read the manuscript. If each member of the special committee signifies his approval within thirty days, the manuscript may be published. If each member of the special committee has not signified his approval within thirty days of the transmittal of the report and manuscript, the Director of Research shall then notify each member of the Board, requesting approval or disapproval of publication, and thirty additional days shall be granted for this purpose. The manuscript shall then not be published unless at least a majority of the entire Board and a two-thirds majority of those members of the Board who shall have voted on the proposal within the time fixed for the receipt of votes on the publication proposed shall have approved.

6. No manuscript may be published, though approved by each member of the special committee, until forty-five days have elapsed from the transmittal of the summary and report. The interval is allowed for the receipt of any memorandum of dissent or reservation, together with a brief statement of his reasons, that any member may wish to express; and such memorandum of dissent or reservation shall be published with the manuscript if he so desires. Publication does not, however, imply that each member of the Board has read the manuscript, or that either members of the Board in general, or of the special committee, have passed upon its validity in every detail.

7. A copy of this resolution shall, unless otherwise determined by the Board, be printed in each copy of every National Bureau book.

(Resolution adopted October 25, 1926, and revised
February 6, 1933, and February 24, 1941)

The Impact of Government on Real Estate Finance in the United States

MILES L. COLEAN

FINANCIAL RESEARCH PROGRAM

STUDIES IN URBAN MORTGAGE FINANCING

National Bureau of Economic Research

Author's Acknowledgments

The author is much indebted to those who read the manuscript of this study during its preparation. Especial gratitude is owed to Professor Richard R. Powell, C. Reinold Noyes, and Professor Arthur H. Cole for their careful review and criticism of the legal and historical aspects of the first several chapters. Professor R. J. Saulnier, the Director of the Financial Research Program, has been a continuous source of aid and encouragement. My thanks are due also to Miss Katherine Krenning for her thorough checking of references and other details of the manuscript.

In a pioneering work on such a controversial subject as that of government intervention, the author must, however, relieve all those who have helped him from any responsibility for his interpretation of the economic and political processes he has examined.

Miles L. Colean

Preface

This study of the influence of government on real estate finance is one of the monographs being prepared under the Urban Real Estate Finance Project of the Financial Research Program. Others deal with the economic characteristics of real estate as they affect its financing and with the mortgage lending activities of the principal public and private agencies active in this segment of the financial system.

In each of the monographs dealing with lending agencies the legal conditions directly affecting their credit extensions will be examined, but in the present study the whole broad range of law and regulation affecting real estate finance is reviewed. To accomplish this difficult task, the author traces the historical development of government's impact on real estate and its financing, showing how it has grown out of the evolving, changing, and not infrequently conflicting objectives of government. These objectives have included, in some cases concurrently, the promotion of small, individual freehold estates, the relief of distresssed mortgage debtors, the protection of depositors and other claimants on the assets of mortgage lending institutions, the encouragement of an adequate flow of investment into real estate and construction, and the provision of adequate housing for selected groups. The author shows how certain steps in this legislative development had to be taken primarily because of the need for mitigating unexpected and unwanted effects of earlier legislative efforts. This account of the legal framework within which mortgage financing is conducted today provides an essential background for the more specialized studies that will follow.

The Urban Real Estate Finance Project is being carried on by the National Bureau of Economic Research under grants of funds from the Association of Reserve City Bankers, the Life Insurance Investment Research Committee, acting for the American Life Convention and the Life Insurance Association of America, and the Rockefeller Foundation.

R. J. Saulnier
Director, Financial Research Program

February 1950

ix

Contents

Introduction

The purpose of this volume is to describe the ways in which government influences the financing of real estate activity and to evaluate the significance of these influences on the flow of funds into real estate investment. It is well to recognize, however, that the ways in which governmental influence is exerted are so numerous, and of so widely varying a degree of directness, that comprehensive treatment, if possible at all, cannot be encompassed in a single study. Government influences real estate financing directly by the regulation and supervision of institutions that make mortgage loans, by the procedure it prescribes for transfer and foreclosure, by the protections it offers to the parties to real estate transactions, and by its own lending and subsidizing activities. At the same time it exerts a less direct influence through those of its policies and actions that affect investment generally and particularly the greater or lesser attractiveness of real estate as against other types of investment. Moreover, the financing of real estate is affected by all those influences bearing upon the rights of property in land and its appurtenances, upon the uses to which land may be put, upon the manner in which these uses may be exercised and the improvements to land accomplished, upon the amount and continuity of income that may be derived from land, and even upon the security of income of those who use real estate as consumers.

Thus, the whole law of real property exerts a profound influence on real estate investment. Building, sanitary and occupancy codes, zoning and planning laws, conservation measures—all have a direct impact upon the value of land and its improvements and hence upon investment in them. The same is true of any legislation affecting the construction industry, from the licensing of contractors and workmen to the policing of monopolistic combinations or the defining of "fair" trade practices.

In a field so vast some limitation of scope must be imposed. It is impossible, for instance, to examine the whole range of fiscal and monetary policies of government, to trace fully the influence exerted by the law of property, or to go deeply into the anti-trust laws or security legislation. On the contrary, an attempt will be made to deal only with the direct and immediate impact of government upon the financing process, making only passing mention of other influences.

The choices that the study makes as to influences to be considered may appear arbitrary in many cases, since there are no unchallengeable criteria for selection. Still, the problem goes beyond a mere question of selection: the association between government and real estate finance is so intimate and of such long standing that the distinction between the governmental and the strictly non-governmental influence is by no means always clear. For example, where can a line be drawn between the influence of the supervisory agency and that of management in respect to the investment policies of lending institutions? Or, what part of mortgage lending risk can be attributed to the characteristics of land and structures as physical objects and what part to legal rights, prohibitions, and procedures? Further, an influence may be so imbedded in custom that it may be recognized only with difficulty and, even then, its significance may not be easily determined.

The problem becomes even more troublesome as we approach the present. Since World War I, and more particularly since the depression that followed it, the influence of government on real estate finance has been vastly intensified and expanded and its source has shifted in the main from state to federal government. This has been accomplished with great speed and amid great controversy and its implications are, for the most part, as yet unrealized. Judgments about these implications call for some forecasting and, consequently, offer a special invitation to the intrusion of personal bias. An effort has been made, however, to describe developments objectively.

The subject matter of this study involves terms that are loosely used, even in legal parlance: real estate, real property, realty, real estate finance, ownership, and so forth.[1] Nevertheless, it is essential to distinguish the physical entity of land, structures and other improvements to land and the various rights and interests of property in land and its appurtenances. Both aspects are of concern to government—the former by way of building codes, zoning ordinances,

1 See C. Reinold Noyes, *The Institution of Property* (New York, 1936) Chapter 5.

flood control, reclamation, and the like, and the latter through the whole body of the law of real property and the credit and tax systems. For our purposes we may take a suggestion tentatively offered by C. Reinold Noyes in *The Institution of Property* which assigns "to the land itself, as object, the term 'realty' and to the interests therein the term 'real property.' " [2] The term "land" will be used synonymously with "realty" and the term "real estate" synonymously with "real property."

The term "real estate finance" is applied to all methods of acquiring real property by purchase or lease, whether by the investment of the funds of the purchaser or lessee, or by the borrowing of funds secured by a mortgage on the property, or by other forms of security. "Owner" is taken to mean a holder of real property in fee simple or a holder of a life interest in real property, and "ownership" applies to a holding in fee simple or for life. The holders of other than life or fee interests will for convenience be referred to as lessees and their holdings as leaseholds. The loose term "equity" will indicate the investment of the owner's or lessee's funds in the property he holds or the value of his holding after satisfying all liens and obligations to which he is subject as owner or lessee. Although these definitions may not satisfy in all respects the niceties of legal disputation, they conform in general to common usage.

The emphasis of the study is on the manner and extent to which investment in real estate is influenced by law and by the administrative policies of government, though the study does not presume to offer a complete history of the impact of government on real estate finance. Nevertheless, the present pattern of influence is so interwoven with legal and political developments of the past that historical excursions are to some extent essential. It is, for instance, impossible to explain today's farm credit arrangements without recalling the course of public land policy; to comprehend the complexities and risks of a mortgage transaction without tracing it, at least briefly, from its medieval source; or to understand the present

---

[2] *Ibid.*, p. 392. The term "land" in the definition includes, of course, all appurtenances and improvements. The definition quoted is later dropped (*ibid.*, p. 396) for one of greater precision, in which the term "realty" is replaced by the term "land" and the term "real property" by the phrase "property with regard to land." It is felt, however, that what may be gained in precision is, for our purpose, lost in simplicity.

concern of government with individual welfare, except in the light
of earlier interventions in times of distress. The primary concern
of the study, however, is in the conditions and influences that prevailed in the 1930's and 1940's, and the account deals mainly, therefore, with developments during these decades, concluding with the
measures passed by the first session of the Eighty-first Congress and
by the state legislatures through 1949. The concluding date of the
study, however, by no means indicates the concluding date of the
processes that are described.

CHAPTER 1

The Background

of Governmental Intervention

THE primary impact of government on real estate finance is through the law of real property, the main body of which is rooted in the law of medieval England. Aside from the stamp of French law on the law of Louisiana, and the remnants of Spanish usage still found in a few of the southwestern states, the English legal tradition is the dominant influence on the relationship between government and real estate and the financing of real estate in this country.

Most of the legal terms that we apply to real property are of English origin. Many of them had been invented and had begun to acquire their present meanings by the end of the thirteenth century. Present forms of land ownership had evolved by that time. Procedures for passing title, granting leases, and giving and taking a mortgage were already well developed. It is not essential to discuss the origins of these concepts, forms, and practices, or to trace in detail their pre-colonial development.[1] It is essential, however, to recognize that they were the expression of a society in which economic and political institutions were closely related, in which the dependent nature of the ownership of real property was well established, and where the law of property had been shaped by the agrarian interest.

With varying emphasis, these characteristics have remained influential to the present time, sometimes because of the obstacles that they presented to changing economic requirements and sometimes, quite to the contrary, because of the very force that an

[1] For an account of the development of the legal background, see C. Reinold Noyes, *The Institution of Property* (New York, 1936) Chapter 3 and, for more extended treatment, Sir Frederick Pollock and Frederic William Maitland, *History of English Law Before the Time of Edward I* (Cambridge, 1923); Frederic William Maitland, *Domesday Book and Beyond* (Cambridge, 1897); and Kenelm Edward Digby, *An Introduction to the History of the Law of Real Property* (Oxford, 1897).

1

ancient tradition, revived and refurbished, gave to a new trend in government policy.

THE AGRARIAN BIAS

Perhaps the most continuously present of the influences that determine current financial practices is the agrarian bias of the law of real property. The law was nurtured in an agricultural society. The mark of the landed interest is clear from the recording of tenures in the Domesday Book of William the Conqueror to the restrictions on alienation in the Magna Charta, the clarification of transfer procedures and contingent responsibilities in the Statute of Quia Emptores (1290), the legalizing of valid equitable rights in land by the Statute of Uses (1535), and the abolition of military tenures in the Statute of Charles II (1660). This interest was fundamentally noncommercial in outlook, and the idea of realty as an article of commerce was foreign to it. Its law was concerned with the determination and fixing of the holding of real property, and was designed to insure the holder in his tenure, to define his rights and duties, and to protect him from fraudulent dispossession. Consistent with these attitudes, the transfer of real property came to be surrounded by an elaborate and tedious procedure involving search and verification, observance of forms and use of language.

This procedure may not have been badly suited to a society in which transfers were comparatively few, in which landholding represented at least as much the assumption of responsibility as it did the prospect of income, and in which trading in land in any modern sense was repugnant, if not unknown. But a number of innovations in transfer procedure accompanied the growing commercialization of society and the increasing mobility of the population and turnover in property ownership. The Statute of Frauds (1677) required transfers of ownership, as well as leases for more than three years' duration, to be in writing,[2] and from the earliest settlements in this country provision was widely made for the recording of deeds.[3] Justice Story notes the relative simplicity of

[2] The requirement of a "sufficient writing" applies also to grants of life interests and other estates less than a freehold and now generally to all leases of more than a year's duration, the term of lease to which the requirement applies varying among the states. See Herbert Thorndike Tiffany, *A Treatise on the Modern Law of Real Property* (new abridged ed., Chicago, 1940) pp. 64 and 670 ff.

[3] George L. Haskins, "The Beginnings of the Recording System in Massachusetts," *Boston University Law Review*, Vol. 21, No. 1, January 1941, p. 281.

American land transfer procedures compared with those of the England of his time, indicating an effort to adapt the law to the requirements of a more fluid society.[4] The rectilinear survey system, as adopted in the Ordinance of 1785,[5] further simplified transfer by reducing the task of legal description; and, for city lots, simplification came also from reference to recorded subdivision plats.

These measures facilitated the transfer of real property and reduced the risk of fraud and error in such transactions. At the same time new difficulties were introduced. Dispersion of ownership and frequency of turnover added to the bulk and complexity of the records and to the task of assuring the validity of claims to rights in real property. The necessity for laborious title investigation still remains, and every time the property is transferred or mortgaged, each link of the chain, normally extending for fifty or sixty years, must be reviewed.

COMPLEXITY OF TITLE PROCEDURES

It is in the process of transfer that the ancient lineage of the law is manifested most plainly. Are there easements or rights-of-way that must be honored? Have dower rights been released? Is there any delinquency in taxes? Do undischarged liens of any sort exist? Is there an unexpired lease binding on the purchaser or a life interest that would deprive the purchaser of the possession of, or revenue from, the property? Is the property zoned to permit the type of use intended? Are there other governmental regulations that would interfere with its development? Does the seller actually have the power to grant a title, or is his interest less than a freehold, being limited to a life interest or subject to the agreement of others who share in his rights?

Few if any such involved considerations apply to the transfer of other types of property; and the precautions that must be taken and the tedious process at each transfer of title put real estate in a special place among the articles of commerce. The buyer of realty

4 Joseph Story, *Commentaries on the Constitution of the United States* (Boston, 1891) Vol. 1, § 174.

5 For a description of the rectilinear system, see Thomas Corwin Donaldson, *The Public Domain, Its History With Statistics* (Washington, 1884) Chapter 7; also, Frank M. Johnson, *The Rectangular System of Surveying* (Land Service Bulletin, Washington, April 1918).

must satisfy himself by an investigation of all the wills, marriages, deeds, liens, judgments, covenants, subdivisions, devises, and other events and documents through which the property has been transferred, mortgaged, or leased over a long period of time to make sure that the chain of title is unbroken and no probability of an adverse claim exists. Since the process is long and laborious, transfer cannot be rapid and, since it is intricate, it always contains an element of risk.

While this system has provided a living for a legion of attorneys, abstractors, and title insurers, it is less satisfactory to the sellers and buyers of real estate. It has been estimated that the cost of such services as appraisal, survey, title search, title insurance, legal counsel, recording and filing, notary, and so forth, will average from 2 to 3 percent of the price of a typical residential property and, proportionately, the cost is heaviest on small transactions.[6]

Furthermore, the whole process takes much time, even months, during a period of great activity.[7] Because of the uncertainty of title until an investigation has been completed, two steps are required: first, a binding contract of purchase and sale must be entered into, contingent only on proof of title, and then, after the investigation is complete and the evidence acceptable, a deed, which supersedes the contract, is executed and the actual transfer takes place.

The substitution of a system of official title registration for the present systems of private title examination has been advanced as a means for reducing the cost and speeding up the process of transfer. Generally known as the Torrens System, title registration provides that, once registered, title defects cannot result in damage or loss to the titleholder, and that any person who has been deprived of a valid interest in the property because of registration is reimbursed from a fund created under the statute. Such methods of registration are widely used in Central Europe, Australia, New Zealand, Canada, in parts of England and Ireland, and in other areas of the British Empire. In the United States, twenty states and Hawaii have authorized title registration systems, but the enabling legislation has been repealed in four states, and, in a fifth, no sys-

6 Miles L. Colean, *American Housing* (The Twentieth Century Fund, New York, 1944) p. 216.
7 Horace Russell, "Private Housing Legal Problems," *Housing, the Continuing Problem* (National Resources Planning Board, Washington, December 1940) p. 62.

tem has been established under the authorization.[8] In all cases the registration systems have been permissive rather than compulsory and, in general, have been very little used. The mere permissive use of such a system, of course, can produce no great result. Since the initial registration is both tedious and costly, there is little inducement to take the first step. It is generally held that title registration could be satisfactorily established only if the system were made compulsory and at least part of the initial cost borne by the state.[9]

In the meantime, the ancient methods generally continue in force; and the risk, the cost, and the loss of time imposed by them exert a special influence on the financing of real property. Real estate financing becomes a process requiring special knowledge and judgment and it is kept apart from the general stream of capital operations. As we shall more and more see, it is also kept at a frequent disadvantage with other forms of activity in its competition for investment funds.

The slowness of legal development has aroused more concern in urban than in rural real estate financing. With the former, an inexpensive and fast-moving procedure is especially needed in order to reduce cost (particularly in the financing of small houses) and to bring real estate operations into the tempo of other commercial and industrial enterprise. At the outset of inquiry, therefore, we find an important impediment to financing arising from a governmental relationship.

THE BIAS TOWARD INDIVIDUAL OWNERSHIP

In the United States the agrarian bias has from the beginning been supplemented by a strong predisposition toward individual, fee simple ownership. Much groundwork for the evolving American

[8] Richard R. Powell, *Registration of the Title to Land in the State of New York* (New York, 1938).

[9] Proponents of the Torrens System claim that, after initial registration, transfer of title is both quicker and less expensive than the present method (see H. T. Tiffany, *op. cit.*, Chapter 32, also H. Russell, *op. cit.*, pp. 64-65). This position is challenged by R. R. Powell (*op. cit.*, p. 74), who concludes, after an analysis of experience under the Torrens System, that it "involves difficulties, expenses, and personnel problems more troublesome and more irremediable than those encountered in recordation." As an alternative, he suggests a system of registration of a possessory title by the person in possession, which could be done with little cost or formality. After a specified period of years for filing adverse claims, this possessory title would become a registered ownership.

policy had already been laid in England. Prohibitions on alienation had been ended for 400 years, and feudal services were abolished by the time settlement got in full swing (1660). Despite
efforts to re-establish the anachronism of feudal tenures in the
proprietary colonies, none of these plans met with success.[10] Story
notes as a remarkable circumstance the almost total absence of
leasehold estates in our colonial history.[11] Only in the Hudson
Valley was anything strongly resembling the manorial system successfully re-established for any length of time. Even in the South,
where large estates were most often found, the plantation operated
directly by the owner displaced the manor operated through an
elaborate system of tenancy.

By the end of the Revolution, with the general abolition of
entailed estates and primogeniture, further steps toward the dispersion of fee simple ownership were taken.[12] The Ordinance of
1787,[13] which organized the Northwest Territory, carried the movement immeasurably further. This ordinance set the foundation for
the law of real property in the states formed from the Territory
by preventing primogeniture, determining the method of inherit-
ance, and providing for devices by will. The principles it enunciated were not only widely adopted in public land states, but also
influenced modifications of the law in the older states. "This statute
struck the keynote of our liberal land policy," comments Joseph
S. Wilson (Commissioner of the Land Office, 1860-61): "The doctrine of tenure is entirely exploded; it has no existence. Though
the word may be used for convenience, the last vestige of feudal
import has been torn from it. The individual title derived from the
Government involves the entire transfer of the ownership of the
soil. It is purely allodial, with all the incidents pertaining to that
title . . ."[14]

Although Commissioner Wilson's enthusiasm on the score of

10 T. C. Donaldson, *op. cit.*, pp. 467, 469; Alfred N. Chandler, *Land Title Origins*
(New York, 1945) Chapter 17.

11 J. Story, *op. cit.*, Vol. 1, § 172.

12 T. C. Donaldson, *op. cit.*, p. 159. An entailed estate, according to Bouvier's Law
Dictionary, is a "fee abridged or limited to the issue, or certain classes of issue, instead of descending to all the heirs."

13 Congress of the Confederation, July 13, 1787. See *Documents of American
History*, Henry Steele Commager, ed. (New York, 1943) Vol. 1, pp. 128 ff; T. C. Donaldson, *op. cit.*, pp. 153 ff.

14 Quoted in T. C. Donaldson, *op. cit.*, pp. 158-59.

completely unconditional ownership requires some qualification,
the importance of the Ordinance to all subsequent law and policy
relating to real property cannot be overestimated. Only one influence was more profound: the existence of a vast, unexploited
national domain.

With the cession of the western lands to the federal government
during and after the Revolution, the means were at last granted for
embodying the ideal of a nation of individual freeholders. For
nearly a hundred years, under the spur of such leaders as Jefferson,
Benton, and Andrew Johnson, the main force of governmental
intervention in the field of our interest was aimed at making land
available to all who were hardy enough to take it. No other single
influence has more profoundly affected the environment and
course of real estate finance in the United States. The land policy
largely determined the kind of security and the type of borrower
with which the financial system would have to deal. In doing so,
it not only made its impress on the system itself but also shaped the
development of future attitudes and action on the part of government. It is necessary, therefore, to trace the growth of American
land policy in some detail.

The ideal of individual freeholds did not come full-blown,
however, nor was it even approached without overcoming natural
and political impediments. The transformation of a wilderness into
a productive community required labor, capital, organization, and
promotion. Outside of New England, colonial governments did
little to aid settlement, this task being mainly left to private endeavor. Later, when the national government took jurisdiction
over the public domain, the same situation largely obtained. Aside
from protection—usually inadequate—against hostile Indians, provision for surveys, and reservation of salt springs for general use,
there was no coddling of the settler. For a long time, even the land
office was remote from places of settlement. Public improvements
fostered by the government usually followed rather than preceded
settlement.

The lack of governmental preparation for, and supervision of,
settlement created a place for land companies—speculative associations created for profit in promoting settlement. Whatever the
fairness of complaints laid against them, land companies undoubtedly performed an important function in the actual promotion of

settlement.[15] These loosely organized associations assumed the task
of exploration and were often able to direct settlers to better lands
than they could find themselves. They supplemented the public
survey system; they settled title claims; they sometimes made provision for defense.

In addition to performing such functions, the land companies
and other large purchasers had another attraction for the early
federal government—they supplied revenue. The argument that
wilderness land was no-rent land, without value until settlement
had taken place, appealed at first only to the settlers themselves.
The new federal government took a different view. Although
wilderness land had to some extent previously been granted without cash consideration, the sale of crown, proprietary, and charter
land for a price had been common during the colonial period.[16]
For the infant republic, land was the resource that appeared most
readily transmutable into revenue; and large buyers seemed more
likely to yield the needed cash than individual settlers.

The principle of sales for revenue was embodied in the first
public land act, the Ordinance of 1785.[17] It was so explicitly enunciated in 1790 by Alexander Hamilton in his *Report on Public
Lands* that it prevailed as a governing influence on the land policy
even beyond the Jacksonian revolution.[18] The Land Act of 1796,[19]
the first enacted under the Constitution, strongly favored the large
grantee in its high minimum price of two dollars an acre, its high
minimum purchase of 160 acres, and its abandonment of the re-

15 Shaw Livermore, *Early American Land Companies* (The Commonwealth Fund,
New York, 1939). See also Benjamin H. Hibbard, *A History of the Public Land
Policies* (New York, 1924) Chapters 3, 4, 12, and 28; and Ray Allen Billington,
Western Expansion (New York, 1949) especially Chapters 8-12.

16 T. C. Donaldson, *op. cit.*, p. 467; Roy M. Robbins, *Our Landed Heritage—The
Public Domain, 1776-1936* (Princeton, 1942) p. 7.

17 Congress of the Confederation, May 20, 1785. *Journals of the Continental Congress*, John C. Fitzpatrick, ed. (Washington, 1933) Vol. 28, pp. 375 ff.

18 Alexander Hamilton, *Report on Public Lands*, American State Papers—Public
Lands (Washington, 1832) Vol. 1, p. 8; T. C. Donaldson, *op. cit.*, p. 198; B. H. Hibbard, *op. cit.*, Chapter 1. Hamilton's objectives in this issue have often been too
narrowly interpreted. R. M. Robbins, *op. cit.*, p. 14, states: ". . . . it would seem
that Hamilton desired not only to use the public domain as an important source of
revenue for the United States Treasury, but also to dispose of it in such a way as
to guarantee a stable economic order." Hamilton proposed that lots of no more than
100 acres be sold at 30 cents an acre (much less than the finally established price)
with larger tracts at a higher figure—*ibid., passim.*

19 Stat. 464 (1796).

quirement of settlement, which had been characteristic even of large grants in colonial times.

The long debate over the questions of grants for revenue as against grants primarily for settlement, and of grants to wholesale purchasers as against small plots to settlers, continued for more than half a century. During that period the weight of the argument gradually shifted. In a succession of measures the price was reduced, the minimum size of the plot was decreased, and the terms of purchase were varied, all with the purpose of favoring the settler over the wholesale buyers.[20] Particularly important in this development was the Preemption Act of 1841,[21] which set four principles as guides to future land policy: (1) the settlement of the public domain was more desirable than revenue; (2) the domain should not fall into the hands of those already amply possessed of land; (3) the domain should be settled in small farms; and (4) the settler should be "protected from all intrusion and allowed a reasonable time to earn or gather together a sum sufficient to buy the land." [22]

Government policy, however, was never wholly consistent. Throughout the main period of land disposal, large grants continued to be made to wholesale buyers; to individuals and states to compensate for internal improvements; to states for the support of education; and to states for general purposes.[23] It was not until the passage of the Homestead Act[24] in 1862 that free land for the settler became a fact. Yet even with the hard-sought goal thus finally established in law, the practice of making large grants was

[20] For an account of the various land acts, see B. H. Hibbard, *op. cit.*, Chapters 4, 15, 17; T. C. Donaldson, *op. cit.*, Chapters 8-30; and Thomas Hart Benton, *Thirty Years' View* (New York, 1854) Vol. 1, Chapters 4 and 70.

[21] 5 Stat. 453 (1841).

[22] R. M. Robbins, *op. cit.*, p. 91.

[23] T. C. Donaldson, *op. cit.*, Chapters 8, 10, 13, 14, and 16.

[24] 12 Stat. 392 (1862). The term "free" as used in connection with the Homestead Act does not imply that settlement, even in absence of a payment to the government, was without expense. The minimum cost of settling an average farm in the middle states in the 1850's has been estimated at $1,000—Clarence H. Danhof, "Farm-Making Costs and the 'Safety-Valve'; 1850-1860," *Journal of Political Economy*, Vol. 49, No. 3, June 1941, p. 325. This estimate takes into account the cost of acquisition, preparation for cultivation, fencing, clearing and breaking land, and the purchase of draft animals, livestock, seed, and implements. Bernard DeVoto (*The Year of Decision, 1846,* Boston, 1943) sets $700 to $1,500 merely for the cost of the family outfit required for crossing the Great Plains.

not abandoned but actually greatly expanded with the inaugura-
tion of grants to railway companies.[25]

EFFECTUATION OF A POLICY

Aside from the argument over revenue, opposition to free land was
continuously offered by the eastern manufacturing interests, who
deplored the dissipation of the labor supply and, later, by the
southern slaveholding interests, who feared the growing predominance of the nonslave area. The political crisis of 1860, which took
the southern states out of the union and thrust the eastern interests
into combination with the West, removed the last barriers to free
entry into the public domain. Within thirty years, the Bureau of
the Census could report that the frontier was closed, and that all
that remained was the filling in of gaps in a settlement broadly
spread over the whole area.[26]

At no time during this development was there effective opposition to a rapid and unrestricted exploitation of the public domain,
although concern was frequently expressed over the potentially ill
effects of unlimited dispersion. Washington feared land sales beyond the possibilities of remunerative settlement, and Jefferson
advocated restraint, but neither had much faith that a policy of
control could be maintained against popular demand for unlimited
access to the public domain.[27] John Quincy Adams, the last ex-
ponent of a system of progressive settlement, had to admit its im-
practicability in face of the political forces of his time.[28]

The land policy, as it was administered, was one of disposal and
diffusion. On the whole, little attention was given to the possibility
that excessively diffused and rapid exploitation of the land might
in the end create serious problems for both the settler and the

25 B. H. Hibbard, *op. cit.*, pp. 241 ff; T. C. Donaldson, *op. cit.*, Chapter 20.

26 See Frederick Jackson Turner, *The Frontier in American History* (New York,
1921) Chapter 1.

27 B. H. Hibbard, *op. cit.*, Chapter 28. The most serious debate on the subject of
orderly settlement along a definite frontier as against unrestricted settlement occurred
in connection with the Act of 1796. The requirement of survey before settlement is
an indication that the former point of view carried some weight. The more liberal
features of the Act of 1800, however, rendered any such control ineffective. See
Samuel Eliot Morison and Henry Steele Commager, *The Growth of the American
Republic* (New York, 1937) Vol. 1, pp. 258-62 and 337.

28 F. J. Turner, *op. cit.*, p. 26.

country as a whole. "On the contrary," says Hibbard,[29] "there seemed to be substantially no apprehension that the settlement could be done in the wrong way, granted only one thing: the ownership of the land should, in the minds of all, be widely diffused. Every other consideration pertaining to the condition of the settler, once he got on to the land, was subordinated, or ignored."

Subsequent changes in the Homestead Act kept the idea of individual family ownership to the fore. "In all these various modifications . . . ," says Proudfit, "the primary conception of the home as the only basis of State and national permanence has been kept intact." [30] Even the practice of making large grants did not seriously interfere with the pursuit of this policy. In almost all cases the major part of the grants to private land companies and to the railroads was rapidly dissipated. The same policy of diffusion of ownership was followed by the older states in the disposal of their own lands and by the new states in respect to the lands distributed to them from the public domain. Further strengthening of the individual ownership concept resulted from the extension of the principle of homestead exemption. Originally designed to preserve the homestead from attachment for debts other than taxes and debts secured by a lien against the premises,[31] the principle has been expanded in thirteen states (up to 1938) to exempt from property taxation all or part of the value of the homestead property.[32] A late reaffirmation was given by President Truman early in 1947: "The long-range agricultural policy of the Government should be aimed at preserving the family-sized farm. . . ." [33] The pattern of farming by independent, if often insecure, small landholders has thus definitely been marked upon the country.

29 B. H. Hibbard, op. cit., p. 551. The effectiveness of using the public domain as an antidote to present and future economic ills received some contemporary questioning. See Arthur M. Schlesinger, Jr., The Age of Jackson (Boston, 1946) pp. 345-46.
30 S. V. Proudfit, Public Land System of the United States (Washington, 1924) p. 5. The Homestead Act of 1860 provided for a maximum free plot of 160 acres. As the difference in farm requirements in semi-arid regions was recognized, the acreage was enlarged to 320 acres (Act of 1909—35 Stat. 639) and then to 640 acres (Act of 1916—39 Stat. 862).
31 See Christopher Gustavus Tiedeman, The American Law of Real Property (St. Louis, 1924) pp. 154-55, or H. T. Tiffany, op. cit., pp. 883-94, for details of the common exemption statutes.
32 H. Russell, op. cit., p. 69.
33 First Economic Report to the Congress, January 1947.

COLLATERAL ASPECTS OF THE LAND POLICY

In its concentration upon the diffusion of ownership the law has been hostile to any development that appeared harmful to individual ownership, and it has, at least until recently, been comparatively neglectful of any feature of real estate activity not directly related to the prime objective.

Note has already been taken of measures adopted in colonial and revolutionary days against the perpetuation, if not against the building up, of huge landed estates. The successful resistance to the reinstitution of feudal tenures, the generally unfavorable attitude toward the maintenance of large estates, and the law of descent which was adopted for the Northwest Territory and accepted in the states created from it, all contributed to the advancement of the main policy. Serving the same end was the early, widespread hostility of the law to the ownership of land by corporations—a hostility that found its precedent in the ancient English Statutes of Mortmain that forbade the transfer of land to the church without a license from the sovereign.[34] This policy, first designed to maintain the King's feudal benefits and controls, was later broadened on social and economic grounds to discourage the accumulation and perpetuation of incorporated estates.

It became a settled principle of American jurisprudence that a corporation might not be created for the purpose of acquiring and holding real property unless the statute under which it is to be organized expressly authorized corporations for such purposes.[35] Consequently both state constitutions and state incorporation acts were generally very specific as to the conditions and limitations under which corporations could hold land. In some cases the restrictions have been drastic. Until recent years in Massachusetts and Illinois, corporations organized for the purpose of buying, selling, or operating real property for profit were forbidden,[36] and

---

34 7 Edward I, c. 2. This statute was preceded by a less effectual ordinance, 9 Henry III, c. 36, and was followed by successive laws: 13 Edward I, c. 32; 15 Richard II, c. 5; 23 Henry VIII, c. 10. In England, present practice is regulated by the Mortmain and Charitable Uses Act of 1888, as amended by the Act of 1891.

35 William Meade Fletcher, *Cyclopedia of the Law of Private Corporations* (Chicago, 1920) Vol. 1, p. 245. It may be noted that the early "land companies" were not chartered companies or corporations, but were associations of a rather informal character. See S. Livermore, *op. cit.*

36 This prohibition gave rise to the device of the Massachusetts Trust, a form of

even now such a landholding corporation cannot be formed in the District of Columbia.[37] The Maryland and Delaware statutes echo the early doctrine of mortmain in their specific limitations on religious corporations; and in Pennsylvania the doctrine is applicable under the common law of the state.[38]

The variety of specific limitations has been very great. In some states, where landholding corporations are now permitted for urban property, they are still banned in agricultural areas. Or, they may be prohibited for agricultural purposes but not for mining, timbering, or cattle raising. Several states limit the number of years during which land may be held, or the area that may be held or cultivated by a corporation. As a general rule, corporations are prevented from holding more land than is essential for carrying out their corporate purposes, a limitation that prevents corporate land operations except by specific charter provision.[39]

Within the present century there has been some relaxation in the American practice of opposing the ownership of land by corporations, particularly for nonagricultural uses. Corporate ownership, consequently, has become widespread in urban income-producing property, both residential and commercial; and agricultural corporations have become at least a minor factor in farm ownership.[40] It is significant, however, that realty corporations were in

association under which the grant is made to trustees in trust for the several designated members and a certificate of such right to a proportionate part of the beneficial interest is issued by the trustees to the several members. The beneficiaries of such trusts have been held to have the same immunities as shareholders in a corporation. This form of association, until modification in the corporation statutes, was particularly popular in the states mentioned. See W. M. Fletcher, *op. cit.*, Vol. 9, Chapter 66.

[37] District of Columbia Code, tit. 29, § 201. Contrary to frequent practice, the District Code grants very liberal landholding privileges to religious bodies.

[38] Maryland Code, 1935, art. 38 of the Declaration of Rights; Delaware Revised Code 1935 (General Corporation Law) c. 65, § 2 (4). See W. M. Fletcher, *op. cit.*, Vol. 2, p. 2051; and William Mack and Donald J. Kiser, *Corpus Juris Secundum* (Brooklyn, 1940) Vol. 19, § 1089, p. 639.

[39] W. M. Fletcher, *op. cit.*, Vol. 2, pp. 2051-54; *Corpus Juris Secundum*, Vol. 19, pp. 1088-89. For digests of state constitutional provisions and laws covering corporate powers, see *The Corporation Manual*, J. B. R. Smith, ed. (New York, 1944). Corporations are generally permitted to take real estate in enforcing payment of a debt but are usually limited as to the period during which such property may be retained.

[40] There is evidence of this in the income tax statistics. However, there are no satisfactory statistics on the characteristics of realty ownership, so that an adequate valuation of the importance of urban real estate and agricultural corporations cannot be made.

the greatest disfavor during the middle and latter parts of the nineteenth century, the main period of development of the corporate device. This disfavor may account in part for the failure of the corporation to become as common in realty ownership as in other types of economic activity, and it has certainly contributed to the dominance of small individual ownership, particularly of farm lands.

Aside from the gradual removal of restrictions against the corporate ownership of urban land, there is little evidence of specific governmental interest in urban real estate ownership and financing prior to the 1930's, except for the confirmation of titles to town land located in the public domain and provision for the reservation and sale of town sites.[41] The states intervened only to grant charters. Although the government was not directly concerned with urban settlement, the same sentiments regarding individual ownership and the close relationship that prevailed between the farm and the urban subdivision gave urban realty much the same long-term investment characteristics as were true of farm land.

The small holding, whether acquired for speculation or direct use, has, therefore, generally remained characteristic of urban as well as farm land. It is true, of course, that great holdings have frequently been assembled in the towns and cities; but they have been created mainly for profit from sales rather than for income from use, and rarely have endured for more than relatively short periods. The important estates that have endured are usually in accidentally strategic locations in the older cities and date from the early period of urban expansion, before modern transportation broke the limitations previously imposed upon urban dispersion. In short, large capital has not been widely attracted to investment in real property. Of the great American fortunes today, only a few have been derived from, or mainly retained in, real property.[42]

[41] For county seat and town-site acts, see Revised Statutes of the United States, §§ 2258, 2286, 2289, 2380-90. See also T. C. Donaldson, op. cit., Chapter 25 and Paul Wallace Gates, The Illinois Central Railroad and its Colonization Work (Cambridge, 1934) Harvard Economic Studies, Vol. 42, Chapter 7.

[42] Of the sixty wealthiest families listed by Ferdinand Lundberg in America's 60 Families (New York, 1937) pp. 26-27, only five are classed as deriving their wealth in any considerable proportion from real estate investment. It is notable that in all five cases (Field, Astor, Green, Taft, and Higgins) urban rather than farm property was the source of wealth. The effectiveness of the land policy is evident in the disappearance of most of the early landholding families from the front ranks of the wealthy (except as their fortunes were transferred to other fields).

The basic law has, of course, created obstacles to the growth and preservation of such fortunes; but probably more influential than this is the fact that the pecuniary inducements to accumulation of real estate, by comparison with other investment opportunities, have been slight. The availability of land permitted over-extension of settlement in relation to the markets for agricultural products and over-expansion of cities in relation to the need for urban sites, thus giving an uncertain prospect for sustained profits. Small operators were willing to take the great chances that these circumstances imposed; investors who sought more calculable risks looked elsewhere.

THE SPECULATIVE ATTITUDE

Great risks, long chances, the prospect of large rewards, and the frequency of staggering losses are all inherent in colonization and settlement. In this country, at least in the beginning, the chance of gain or loss was left to the participants in the enterprise. Except for making the opportunity possible and, with varying degrees of effectiveness, policing the process, government stood aside. No attempt was made to moderate the risk through governmental intervention until long after the main policy was established. On the contrary, it is probable that by its policy of unrestricted expansion the government actually contributed to the risks that individuals were forced to take.

From the earliest days, consequently, the speculative point of view was deeply impressed upon American land development. It actuated the bold land company enterprises of the colonial period [43] and continued to be a motivating force for as long as the disposal of the public domain was a political issue. Time and again voices were raised against land speculation. Gallatin, both as congressman and as Secretary of the Treasury, attempted to stop it.[44] Benton continually inveighed against it.[45] Speculative acquisition was not limited to the wholesale purchasers. Settlers themselves had the speculative fever; and the practice of taking up more land than could be individually cultivated was common even among small

[43] S. Livermore, *op. cit.*, Introduction by Julius Goebel, Jr., pp. xxiv-xxv.
[44] See B. H. Hibbard, *op. cit.*, pp. 70, 73, and Chapter 12 for a balanced discussion of the contributions as well as the evils of land speculation.
[45] T. H. Benton, *op. cit.*, Vol. 1, particularly Chapters 4 and 70.

buyers. Belief in the inevitable increase in land value early became a key dogma in the American economic credo. Since the holding of land for a rise in price was considered an assured—or nearly assured —means of obtaining wealth, settlers did not hesitate to extend themselves to the limit.[46]

Optimism often outran capacity to pay, as settlers outran the prospects of profitable cultivation. Settlement was at best a grim business, and both its monetary and spiritual rewards were often meager. The prospect of effortless gain through increase in land value took away some of the bitterness of a hard life. Though speculators, particularly the large ones, were constantly denounced, it is not too much to say that speculation helped to make the frontier endurable.

The risks that speculation added, however, were grave. It tended to put more land into private hands than could be profitably utilized. The land was generally purchased on credit, and even when cash was paid, or when, under the Homestead Act, the land was obtained free of cost, it was often mortgaged to pay for improvements. Between unlimited entry on the one hand and extensive borrowing on the other, the land structure from the start was economically unstable. Investment in a true sense was extremely hazardous, and, in the speculative sense, losses ran a close race with profits.[47]

In the towns and cities speculation has undoubtedly been on a much wider scale than in rural lands. Town lots became the currency of speculation. Repeated liquidation occurred, but the ardor could be dampened only for short periods.[48] Instability was thus

[46] B. H. Hibbard, op. cit., Chapter 12. P. W. Gates, op. cit., pp. 110-13 analyzes the types of speculators and their motives as follows: small farmers with more land than they could cultivate; small business and professional men investing on the side; eastern capitalists "who wanted to take a flyer," and professional speculators, individuals and corporations, who often took an active part in encouraging settlement and obtaining public improvements. Speculation seems to have been the common denominator of all forms and locales of settlement. See R. A. Billington, op. cit., Chapters 5, 7, 10, 12, and 14.

[47] Witness the wholesale defaults on government land contracts by 1820, and the repeated waves of foreclosures, culminating in the twenty-year depression in farm values following World War I (see Chapter 3).

[48] Aaron Morton Sokolski, The Great American Land Bubble (New York and London, 1932); also Homer Hoyt, A Hundred Years of Land Values in Chicago (Chicago, 1933). According to Hoyt (p. 42), the effect of the 1836-42 panic was "to ruin most of those who had bought land in Chicago prior to 1836." A disaster almost as bad occurred in 1858 (ibid., p. 80). In the 1920's, the subdivision, apartment, and

built into the urban as well as the rural land structure, producing a constant hazard to investment and a constant threat to the security of real estate loans.

The speculative attitude, reared as it was on the concept of unrestricted ownership, added waste and indifference to instability. In agricultural areas, it tended to an extravagance with land resources by owners who frequently found moving cheaper than conservation, and by tenants whose interest in a particular plot was even less than that of the owner. In cities, it justified an intensification of use that was limited only by the rapidly expanding potentials offered by building science and, more markedly than in the country, bred unconcern for the general welfare. Some of these forces might have spent themselves with relatively little harm, or, indeed, never have been so fully developed, had they not operated in conjunction with a rate of population increase new in the world's history. Between 1800 and 1860 rural population quadrupled and urban population grew twenty-four fold. Between 1860 and 1900, rural population doubled and urban population quadrupled.[49] Such growth and expansion created an optimism for the future that blinded people to the difficulties that were steadily being engendered.

THE RESURGENCE OF SOCIAL CONTROL

Thus, through the nineteenth century the main role of government was what might be called intervention in reverse. The federal land acts, through which the public domain was dissipated, state and federal grants for roads and canals, and railroad grants were all parts of a policy of induced exploitation which, as we shall observe, left its mark on every phase of real estate investment. Primarily, it decreed an investment system based on numerous small holdings, the holders of which were constantly in need of credit. Secondly, the policy was carried out with a minimum regard for economic considerations and often in flagrant disregard of its social implications.

---

office building booms characteristic of Miami, Detroit, Chicago, Los Angeles, New York, etc., provide still vivid evidence of the ardor for, as well as the losses from, realty speculation.

49 See Arthur Meier Schlesinger, *Paths to the Present* (New York, 1949) Chapter 11; also, by the same author, *The Rise of the City, 1878-1898*, A History of American Life (New York, 1933) Vol. 10.

The stage was now set for a revival of the dormant concept of the superior rights of the state to those of individual owners, for the purpose both of giving them protection and of guiding their activity. This gradual reassertion took numerous forms. The law of nuisance and the police power underwent a great transformation. The power of the state as landlord was belatedly brought into positive application in areas where recourse to it was still possible; and the power of eminent domain was expanded to achieve ends never before considered to be within the meaning of public purpose. The numerous ways in which government may exert influence and control over credit and lending institutions were brought into play so as to make of credit an all-purpose instrument for the control of real estate investment and development. The taxing power, always of profound influence on real estate activity, was applied as a means of directing the course of activity. The spending power was lavishly used to the same end. Finally, the development and application of the doctrine of reserved emergency powers furnished the means through which purposes might be achieved that were beyond attainment by the exercise of the powers previously listed. The remaining chapters of this study deal with these developments as they brought about within a short space of time a union of the political and economic systems as thorough, if not always as happy, as that which prevailed when the basic concepts of real property first found effective expression.

Governmental Influence on the Use

of Real Property

A N especially noteworthy area in which governmental intervention has steadily expanded is that concerned with the methods
by which land is utilized and buildings are constructed, occupied,
and maintained. There are several objectives in this form of
intervention. Beginning with the provision of access and the prevention of hazards and nuisances,[1] the government's aim has been
broadened in the course of years to provide a measure of protection
to the landholder against his own acts and, beyond this, to include
moral and economic, as well as physical, considerations within the
scope of regulation. And now, as a means of counterbalancing the
often wasteful effects of its expansionist land policy, government
has asserted its powers to prevent land misuse. Although these objectives may not be immediately concerned with the financing of
real estate, they are nonetheless vital to it. In many ways, the control that the law imposes upon physical realty determines the value
of property, the yield that may be expected of it, and the security
of investment in it. Physical control of land and of land uses sets
the framework for financing operations no less than the legal
strictures on the rights in real property.

The ability of government to control land use derives mainly
from the police power, the power of eminent domain, and the
rights of the state as a landowner. All of these powers are vested in
the states and may be exercised directly by them or, through dele-
gation, by their political subdivisions. The federal government
may exercise police power only in situations affecting interstate
commerce and on lands owned by it. In using the power of eminent
domain, it has more limited authority than the states; and its

---

[1] For the development of the nuisance doctrine, see Shirley Adelson Siegel, "Real
Property Law and Mass Housing Needs," *Law and Contemporary Problems*, Vol. 12,
No. 1 (December 1947) pp. 30 ff.

privileges as a landowner were, during the period of their greatest extent, almost wholly unused as a means of controlling land use. The types of intervention discussed in this chapter are, therefore, mainly of state origin. Within the last few decades, however, the federal government, by a broad interpretation of the commerce clause, by use of the spending power, and by more direct and novel means, has increasingly sought on its own initiative to influence land use.

THE POLICE POWER

Under the police power, the state reserves the right to restrict personal liberties and to limit property rights in order to protect the safety, health, morals, and general welfare of the public. Although this power is not new, its scope is still being broadened as the term "general welfare" itself is being broadened to cover a widening range of social and economic considerations. Characteristic of the modern point of view is the decision of a Wisconsin court which held that "the same restrictions (i.e., those imposed in the interest of public health and safety) may be imposed upon the use of property in the promotion of the public welfare, convenience, and general prosperity." [2]

The exercise of the police power involves no responsibility for indemnification by the state. If a particular land use is noxious in the eyes of the law, it may be prohibited, irrespective of the loss to the property owner. Because of this extreme doctrine, the courts have frequently been reluctant to expand the definition of the police power. A further restraint exists in the "due process" clause of the federal constitution, under which the harmfulness of the use must be clearly demonstrated. Nevertheless, the tendency is toward a broader definition.

BUILDING REGULATIONS

The most familiar means of limiting private property rights through exercise of the police power are municipal ordinances regulating the construction and occupancy of buildings. Govern-

2 Carter v. Harper, 182 Wis. 148 (1923). An example of the "convenience and general prosperity" concept will be found in rural zoning, Chapter 2, pp. 27-28. The police power has even been extended to matters of aesthetics: in Washington, D. C., for example, the appearance of buildings fronting on certain main boulevards and public places is subject to the approval of the Commission of Fine Arts (40 U.S.C. 121, c. 400; 53 Stat. 1144, 1939).

ment effort to protect the public from unsafe structures dates back to Babylonian tablets and the laws of ancient Rome.[3] After the fall of Rome there was little attempt to control building until towns were again important, and then regulation was mainly to prevent the spread of fire. Similarly in this country the first regulations related to methods of erecting chimneys.[4] Of all forms of realty control, building codes have the most consistent and uninterrupted development, broadening in scope with successive catastrophes and the increasing congestion of population. In large cities today, nearly all phases of construction, many features of planning (such as window and room sizes, ceiling heights, stair widths, depth of yards, etc.) and many aspects of building occupancy and operation are subject to regulation.

Although this regulatory power rests in the states, only a few, notably Indiana, Ohio, and Wisconsin, have attempted to cover the whole range of building in state codes.[5] Many states, however, maintain at least partial regulation of such structures as hospitals, schools, places of assembly and dwellings, safety measures in factory buildings, and provisions for the sanitation of dairy barns. For the most part, the power is delegated to municipalities with the result that there are some 1,500 to 1,800 building codes, and few of these are duplications.[6]

The codes differ in the subjects they treat and in their manner of treatment. Some relate to building planning and structural requirements only. Many also cover sanitary requirements, but in others the sanitary code is a separate document. Electrical work is often separately handled. Some cities regulate the occupancy of buildings after erection, particularly places of assembly, factories, and tenements. Some phases of building operation, such as seasonal requirements for heat and maintenance of boilers and elevators,

---

3 Frank Burton, *History of Building Codes* (Proceedings, Fifteenth Annual Meeting, Building Officials Conference of America, 1929) p. 41.

4 *Ibid.*, pp. 42-46. Also, Joseph D. McGoldrick, Seymour Graubard, and Raymond J. Horovitz, *Building Regulation in New York City* (The Commonwealth Fund, New York, 1944) p. 27. Other early regulations covered lot line restriction, the authorization of construction, and the materials for roofs.

5 Miles L. Colean, *American Housing* (The Twentieth Century Fund, New York, 1944) p. 125.

6 *Ibid.*, p. 125. George N. Thompson, *Preparation and Revision of Building Codes,* Building Materials and Structures Report BMS19, U.S. Department of Commerce (Washington, 1939).

are regulated in most large cities. Many cities have closing and demolition ordinances, effective where buildings, either beyond repair or in the hands of owners who refuse to repair them, are clearly a menace to health and safety.

The allowable safe strength of timber and steel beams and columns, the load that a brick wall is permitted to carry, the size of windows and rooms, the amount and kind of covering required to fireproof steel members, the width of stair required to discharge a given number of persons, the proper method of venting a plumbing system—all these details, and many more, vary from city to city. Furthermore, there are differences not only in the permitted stresses of materials but also in the allowances for floor loads, weight of snow, and wind pressure to which the stresses are applied.[7]

Since there is no central authority to which cities may look for the establishment of standards, diversity continues to be an outstanding code characteristic, intensifying the local nature of the construction industry, preventing the standardization of many types of product, and probably adding unnecessarily to the cost of construction.[8] The lack of widely accepted standards for the satisfactory performance of the various parts of a structure also slows up technological advance and makes easier the perversion of codes to serve special interests. Both these results tend to maintain, or actually create, artificially high levels of construction cost.

The federal government has tried several methods of bringing its influence to bear on the character of building regulations. Through the National Bureau of Standards of the Department of Commerce, it has carried on research in construction standards and has assisted in developing the model code of the American Standards Association. Through the Housing and Home Finance Agency, a model plumbing code has been prepared, performance requirements for residential construction have been issued, and considerable work done on the formulation of standards for a number of the elements of housing construction.[9] Through the con-

---

7 M. L. Colean, *op. cit.*, p. 127.

8 See Walter J. Mattison, "Building Codes Kill Low Cost Housing," *Municipalities and the Law in Action* (Washington, 1939).

9 Authority to engage in this type of activity was specifically granted to the Housing and Home Finance Agency in the Housing Act of 1948 (62 Stat. 1276) and greatly expanded in the Housing Act of 1949 (Public Law 171, 81st Congress).

struction requirements and housing standards of the Federal Housing Administration, the government has imposed a sort of super-code in so far as the operations of that agency are concerned. In connection with its public buildings and public housing programs, the federal government has also imposed its own standards but, except during the war period, the practice has been mainly to follow local codes in such construction. On occasion the Department of Justice has offered to appear in the role of *amicus curiae* in cases involving allegedly unreasonable code restraints but it has never actually done so. Acting through special powers, federal authorities required modifications of code provisions during the war period as the price of permitting communities to have materials for housing construction.[10] Although similar coercive methods, through the withholding of Federal Housing Administration financing, public housing grants, and so forth, have been suggested for peacetime use, they have never been employed.

Without regulation of the physical character of property, urban realty investment would be very hazardous. Building codes greatly moderate the risk of fire and maintain a minimum standard of construction. They eliminate a great deal of unscrupulous competition that would otherwise detract from the value of sound structures. On the other hand, many elements in present day codes no doubt raise the cost of construction and consequently limit the volume of activity.

In a special study of Chicago, for instance, evidence of an inverse correlation between code rigidity and building activity was discovered.[11] To this extent, investment opportunities will be restricted and hazard may be increased. For another thing, an artifi-

---

10 Wartime construction was required by the federal government to conform to the following: "Critical Construction Materials Design Guide," June 26, 1943, War Production Board; "National Emergency Specifications for the Design, Fabrication and Erection of Structural Steel for Building," September 10, 1942, War Production Board; "National Emergency Specifications for the Design of Reinforced Concrete Buildings," November 10, 1942, including amendment dated March 30, 1944, War Production Board; "National Emergency Specifications for the Design, Fabrication and Erection of Street Grade Lumber and its Fastenings for Buildings," Directive No. 29, August 9, 1943, War Production Board; and "Emergency Plumbing Standards for Defense Housing," February 1942, Division of Defense Housing Coordination, Office for Emergency Management.

11 Howard P. Vermilya, *Building Regulation in Chicago* (Chicago Association of Commerce, Chicago, 1945); also Miles L. Colean, *Your Building Code* (National Committee on Housing Inc., New York, 1946).

cial form of competition may be set up among the communities in
a metropolitan district, since less onerous regulations and lower
building costs in the outlying communities and unincorporated
areas contribute to the dispersion of population and business from
the central areas and to the consequent loss of their property values.

REGULATION OF LAND USE

Although the bulk of our land-use regulation was enacted during
the last few decades, the idea of legally determining the manner of
occupying and utilizing land is far from new. The early New England towns had a considerable degree of regulated planning, and
a number of our important cities, notably Philadelphia, Savannah,
and Washington, have, with varying consistency and continuity,[12]
evolved from official plans. Quite undesignedly, the survey system,
created by the Land Ordinance of 1785, turned out to be the most
significant single planning measure ever embodied in American
law, for it determined the characteristically rectangular physical
pattern not only of the major part of the rural area of the country
but of numerous towns and cities as well.

Several planning or use-control features were embodied in the
early public land acts. The requirement of a government survey
and patent to establish title tended to reduce the scattered, hit-or-
miss settlement so common in parts of the original colonial area,
notably Virginia. The minimum, and sometimes the maximum,
area that might be taken up was regulated. The initial sales price
was regulated. Efforts were made (although without success) to
prevent speculation and to provide for progressive expansion westward. Other measures specifically provided for the disposition of
lands left behind in the first rush of settlement.[13]

As we have noted before, however, the early emphasis was on
expansion, not purposeful control. And, though the Constitution
specified the power to dispose of the public domain according to
any method whatever, the inherent potentialities thus given for
social and economic planning were not even considered, and even
physical planning was only accidentally indulged in.

12 National Resources Committee, *Urban Planning and Land Policies*, Volume
2 of the report of the Urbanism Committee (Washington, 1939) pp. 15-16.
13 9 Stat. 114 (1845-51) Act of August 3, 1846, c. 78, § 5; Revised Statutes, Title
XXXII, § 2455.

The states likewise showed small concern with methods of land utilization during the first hundred years of the Republic. Their interest, like that of the federal government, was in getting people on the land and encouraging the growth of cities. To these ends, state laws encouraged unimpaired freedom of use; and land ownership lost nearly all its ancient responsibilities to the community. For the most part, land-use regulation was left to a later period when a reawakening community consciousness revived some of the old powers and devised several new means of influence or coercion.

SUBDIVISION REGULATION

Among the first reassertions of the power to control land use in cities was the regulation of subdividing. The first of such regulations appears to have been enacted in 1882 when the village of Oak Park, Illinois, required plats to be filed in advance of sale and to conform to certain standards of layout. In 1888, the District of Columbia was authorized to regulate the platting of subdivisions. Since then, all but six states have authorized cities to regulate subdivision practices.[14]

As a minimum, subdivision control requires the filing of a plat showing lot sizes and layout and width of streets to conform with the city requirements. Many cities go further in supervising the planning of the area, specifying the type of improvement—streets, sidewalks, sewers, and water—to be installed, and requiring that these improvements be paid for by the subdivider.[15]

The control is thus qualitative rather than quantitative. No jurisdiction has claimed directly the right to govern the amount of land that may be subdivided; and constitutional considerations have so far prevented the assumption of this power. The requirement for the installation of improvements has, however, a tendency to restrict the development of urban lots to numbers that can be absorbed by the market within a fairly short time. Limited as these

[14] Harold William Lautner, *Subdivision Regulations; An Analysis of Land Subdivision Control Practices* (Public Administration Service, Chicago, 1941) pp. 217-342. National Housing Agency, Office of the General Counsel, *Comparative Analysis of the Principal Provisions of State Subdivision Control Laws Relating to Housing and Urban Development* (Washington, January 1, 1945).

[15] H. W. Lautner, *op. cit.*, p. 246. Usually subdivision control is limited to areas within municipal boundaries, although in some cases areas from three to five miles beyond the city limits (unless impinging on other municipalities) are brought under the regulation.

laws are, they still may stimulate real estate investment by contributing to the orderliness of urban development, assuring reasonable standards of land improvement and public facilities, and requiring that the costs of such improvements be included in the original development instead of overhanging the property as special assessments. On the other hand, these requirements may restrain investment by requiring excessive expenditures and thus have the retarding influence often attributed to building codes.

Subdivision regulation is by no means universal and there are only a few instances where it effectively assures a high standard of neighborhood layout. Therefore, the federal government, as a feature of its mortgage insurance system, has established "neighborhood standards" with which all users of the system must comply. This, like the use of FHA construction requirements, represents an intrusion of the federal government into matters normally under local jurisdiction only, and introduces another element into the already complex framework of control over realty investment.

Allied to these regulations is the use by developers of covenants running with the land, which may, among other requirements, restrict the size of lots and the minimum size or cost of dwellings, establish building lines, prevent inharmonious building, and exclude certain racial groups from tenancy or ownership.[16] Since the covenants depend for their enforcement upon the injunctive power, or the assessment of damages, they show how governmental power can be used to maintain private regulations. Designed to protect investment, they may, by freezing the character of development over a long period, ultimately have the opposite result.

ZONING

Aside from the yard and building line requirements and the fire districting common in building codes, the most widespread method of controlling land use is zoning. This form of regulation involves the division of cities or other political subdivisions into districts according to allowable land use—residential, commercial, indus-

16 The U. S. Supreme Court, in 334 U. S. 24 and 334 U. S. 1, has denied access to the courts for the enforcement of covenants preventing sale or occupancy on the basis of race. Regulations announced late in 1949 by the Federal Housing Administration and the Veterans' Administration deny the availability of insured or guaranteed mortgage financing in any instance where a discriminatory covenant was of record.

trial, and many varieties of each of these. In some cases of county zoning, agricultural uses are stipulated as well.

Urban zoning regulates the area, height, and volume of buildings, although height restriction in some cities antedates zoning. The first zoning ordinance was that of New York City in 1916, following the 1914 enabling act of the New York legislature. Up to the present time, twenty-one states have made possible the enactment of zoning ordinances either in all counties or in specified areas.[17]

The impetus for zoning came from the great congestion of cities following the invention of the skyscraper. The steel frame building permitted an intensity of land use that robbed neighboring properties of light and air, converted streets into dim canyons, and endangered the health and safety of the public. Yet any attempt to interfere with such use of land involved both an intrusion on private rights that had been stoutly asserted and maintained for generations and a spectacular claim of superior community rights.

For a number of years, the principle of zoning had a stormy court history. Nevertheless, the principle tended on the whole to be enlarged by successive court decisions. It is now established and is still being broadened as an instrument for controlling the economic and physical pattern of cities. Although a "nonconforming use" in existence at the time an ordinance was passed is often allowed to remain indefinitely in its privileged position, this is not universally so. Early in the development of zoning theory, the Supreme Court ruled that the banning of a pre-existing, nonconforming use did not take property without due process.[18] Authorities contend that the police power, as supported by this decision, is broad enough to permit retroactive restrictions, especially where a reasonable time is allowed to amortize existing investment.[19] A more drastic proposal (as yet nowhere enacted) would establish a

17 For a thorough discussion of zoning principles and practices, see Edward Murray Bassett, *Zoning* (Russell Sage Foundation, New York, 1940).
18 Hadacheck v. Los Angeles, 239 U. S. 394 (1915); 60 L. ed. 348.
19 E. M. Bassett, *op. cit.*, pp. 112 ff.; Richard T. Ely and George S. Wehrwein, *Land Economics* (New York, 1940) pp. 108-9. In spite of this doctrine, the enabling legislation in many states prevents action against nonconforming uses, and in only a few cities have limits been set on the period during which the nonconforming use may be maintained.

life period for each building at the time of erection, so as to permit greater flexibility in future redistricting.

Although some county zoning in the twenties included districting for agricultural purposes, Wisconsin in 1929 definitely inaugurated rural zoning under which farming (not already established) was prohibited in certain submarginal areas in favor of forestry or recreation.[20] Here the economic, as contrasted with the physical, basis for zoning is undisguised.

OTHER WAYS OF REGULATING LAND USE

Aside from a few planning features in public land laws, the beginnings of subdivision regulation, and a few early instances of planned cities, land-use control during the nineteenth century consisted mainly of the widespread establishment of drainage districts, with powers to lay out drainage systems, to construct works, and to levy taxes or assessments. Irrigation districts, involving a similar legal framework, also became common,[21] but any true concern with land-use control was a later development.

Land-use planning in urban areas, in the sense of a legislatively supported official program for the coordinated development of highways, streets and other transportation facilities, schools and recreational areas, and other public improvements was largely a development of the period 1909 to 1920.[22] Interest was stimulated by the revival in 1901 of the long-neglected plan of the city of Washington, but the chaotic growth of cities following World War I created demands for more comprehensive control of urban expansion. Early city planners generally omitted the possibility of the planned use of privately-owned land from their considerations, except as it might be influenced indirectly by public improvements. Gradually, however, the planning concept has been expanded to include direct guidance of private land use until it has now become one of the important objectives of planning.

20 R. T. Ely and G. S. Wehrwein, *op. cit.*, p. 187.
21 *Ibid.*, pp. 168-71, 264.
22 Such planning had tentative beginnings in the nineteenth and early twentieth centuries. The most noteworthy of the earlier plans, however, were often privately sponsored (as the Chicago plan of 1909) and were without any legal authority through which they could be carried into effect. For the development of official city planning, see Thomas Adams, *Outline of Town and City Planning* (Russell Sage Foundation, New York, 1935) Chapter 9.

Currently, public improvements are planned in relation to, and for their effect on, private land uses, with public works frequently used as a means to attain broad economic and social objectives. Zoning and subdivision regulations are considered elements of the planning function and, at least in their main outlines, are subject to the master plan of the community. The present New York City Charter, for example, represents a thorough-going effort to centralize all aspects of urban planning activity.[23]

EMINENT DOMAIN APPLIED TO PLANNING

Growing concern with slums has created another field for official land-use planning. Although the police power, if effectively invoked, can require the vacation or demolition of unsafe and unsanitary structures, it cannot affect title to property, nor can it require the wholesale reorganization of an area. The redevelopment of outworn districts called for something more than the police power, namely, the authority to liquidate old ownerships, to wipe out old property lines, and to redistribute land in a manner conforming to new requirements. The power of eminent domain answered these requirements, but its application for such broad objectives demanded a much modified definition of "public purpose." Both federal and state courts have complied and the power of states, or their instrumentalities, to condemn land to provide sites for publicly-owned housing has been upheld in several decisions.[24]

23 The New York City Charter was established by a referendum vote in 1936. For a description of its planning features, see Edward Murray Bassett, *The Master Plan* (Russell Sage Foundation, New York, 1938) Chapter 14.

24 The power of the federal government to take land for public housing purposes was denied by the Circuit Court of Appeals, Sixth Circuit, October 9, 1935. The United States v. Certain Lands in City of Louisville, 78 F (2d) 684; 296 U. S. 567; 297 U. S. 726. Later cases casting doubt on this decision are: (1) Oklahoma City v. Sanders, 94F (92d) 323 (January 8, 1938) and (2) the City of Cleveland v. the United States of America and Federal Public Housing Authority; and John J. Boyle, et al. v. the United States of America and Federal Public Housing Authority, 323 U. S. 329; 89 L. ed. 274 (January 2, 1945). The author is indebted to Mr. David Krooth, formerly General Counsel of the Federal Public Housing Authority for the following comment on these cases:

"In the Louisville case, the Court held that the National Industrial Recovery Act, so far as it attempted to authorize the Government to condemn private property for low-cost housing and slum clearance projects, and for the purpose of reducing unemployment, was unconstitutional, since such is not a public use and is not authorized by the General Welfare Clause of the Constitution.

"In the Oklahoma case, which was not a condemnation proceeding, the Court

Decisions in the courts of the District of Columbia, Illinois, and
New York have approved the use of condemnation proceedings
even where the purpose was not the redevelopment of the area by
a public agency or for residential use, holding that slum removal
in itself was a sufficient service to the public interest.[25] Since the
reassembly of large urban tracts is rarely possible without a resort
to condemnation, the new interpretation gives government a strong
weapon to use in determining the conditions of investment in an
ever-expanding proportion of the urban area. New York has gone
even further in providing instruments for the control of future
land use. The new state constitution of 1938 gave to municipalities
the power to acquire "by purchase, gift, eminent domain, or otherwise" any land considered necessary for a housing program even
though not necessary for current requirements.[26] This provision
was reinforced by specific legislation.[27]

The establishment of the doctrine that private land might be
taken for the purpose of clearing slums and placing the land in
condition for re-use inaugurated a series of state "urban redevelopment" laws. These, along with the federal aid that was provided to

of Appeals held that public housing and slum clearance was for a public and governmental purpose and therefore constitutional.

"In the Cleveland case, which involved the tax exemption of a PWA project
acquired by the Government by eminent domain under the provisions of the National
Industrial Recovery Act, the Supreme Court of the United States held that the United
States Housing Act was constitutional and was enacted pursuant to the Welfare
Clause of the Constitution, and that the project was exempt from taxes. This case
reverses the principle of law upon which the Louisville case is based.

"It is now generally admitted by the Bar that public housing and slum clearance
come within the delegated powers of the Federal Constitution.

"Despite these later decisions, the Federal Government, in the pursuit of its public housing program, has not directly taken land but has financed local authorities,
which in turn have used the condemnation power. The exercise of eminent domain
by such local agencies has not been effectively challenged, and the legality of the
practice seems now firmly established."

25 See U. S. Supreme Court, Minnie Keys v. U. S., 119 Fed. (2d) 444, October 13,
1941; Supreme Court of Illinois, John F. Zurn v. The City of Chicago, et al., 389
Ill. 114, 59 NE (2) 18 (1945), October 17, 1945; New York Court of Appeals, Mary
V. Murray, et al., v. LaGuardia, et al., December 2, 1943; New York Supreme Court,
Pratt v. LaGuardia, et al., March 17, 1944.

26 New York Constitution, art. 18, § 9.

27 New York Laws 1945, c. 887. For broad interpretations of the public purpose
concept, see also S. A. Siegel, op. cit., pp. 39-41, and Myres S. McDougal, "Municipal
Land Policy and Control," Annals of the American Academy of Political and Social
Science, Vol. 242 (November 1945) pp. 91-92.

spur the movement, are discussed in a later chapter, since they are so distinctly a part of the interventionary pattern of the years following World War II.

In effect, these and the public housing measures brought a restoration of the power of the state as landlord, making it potentially an important force in urban real estate investment. The same restoration was occurring in rural areas. In several of the states, the recovery of rural land, particularly through tax foreclosure, resulted in more positive use of ownership power; and the federal government also, on that part of the public domain that was left, as well as on lands reacquired by default or purchase, began a conscious direction of land use by means of irrigation projects, control of grazing, timbering control, and reforestation.

Governmental Influence on Rural Land Use

The broadening of the planning concept and the power to effectuate planning programs has not been solely an urban phenomenon. As the frontier narrowed, the attention of state governments, and, more particularly, of the federal government, turned to problems of the preservation of resources remaining in the public domain and of the more economic utilization of land that had passed into private hands.

Some of the first moves along these lines—the undertakings in drainage and irrigation mentioned above—were privately initiated within the framework of state law; but government soon adopted direct means of intervention. At first, the federal effort was only to stimulate state action; thus, vast areas of swamp or arid lands were transferred to states that would agree to undertake drainage or irrigation works.[28] But so many local drainage districts had fallen into financial difficulties by 1933 that the federal government came to their aid with Reconstruction Finance Corporation loans.[29] At an earlier date (1902), Congress began to provide funds for the installation of irrigation works on public lands in seventeen western states, with the idea that settlers would eventually reimburse the government through the payment of water charges—a prospect

[28] Thomas Corwin Donaldson, *The Public Domain, Its History With Statistics* (Washington, 1884) Chapters 12 and 30; Benjamin H. Hibbard, *A History of the Public Land Policies* (New York, 1924) Chapters 14 and 20.
[29] Reconstruction Finance Corporation Act, 47 Stat. 5 (1932); 15 U.S.C. 601 *et seq.*

only partly realized. As the program developed, reclamation projects were extended to provide electric power, to assist in flood
control and navigation, and to supply water for domestic and
industrial purposes as well as to serve irrigation requirements.[30]

Reclamation began to add thousands of acres to the supply of
farm land shortly before it was realized that the supply was already
too great for economic operation. As new acreage was created, the
federal government undertook through other means, such as the
"rural resettlement" program of the thirties, to acquire already
settled land and withdraw it from cultivation.[31] This confusion in
land policy is still far from being resolved.

The conservation and use programs of the Department of Agriculture represent another form of governmental land-use regulation. These programs began with the public recognition of the
waste of resources resulting from the exploitative cultivation of
private lands. Before the first World War, Kansas and Texas attempted to deal with erosion problems,[32] but it remained for the
drought and the depression of the middle thirties to highlight the
problem. In 1935, Congress passed the Soil Conservation Act,[33]
authorizing the use of public funds in the rebuilding of land in
local conservation districts set up under appropriate state laws. By
1947, almost three million farms and ranches, comprising 63 percent of the nation's cropland, were receiving federal assistance
under this program; and allotments under the program for that
year totaled $245 million.[34] This influence on farm values is not
easy to measure, but it is unquestionably substantial.

FROM FLOOD CONTROL TO REGIONAL PLANNING

The protection of private lands from flood damage shows an historical shift from private, through state, to federal jurisdiction,
much the same as in the case of irrigation activities. Originally such
protection was a private responsibility. In the original French

30 R. T. Ely and G. S. Wehrwein, *op. cit.,* pp. 265 ff.; *Federal Register,* Vol. 11,
No. 177, pt. 2 (1946) p. 297.
31 This operation is now carried on by the Soil Conservation Service. See *Federal
Register,* Vol. 11, No. 177, pt. 2 (1946) p. 297.
32 R. T. Ely and G. S. Wehrwein, *op. cit.,* p. 219.
33 49 Stat. 163 (1935); 16 U.S.C. 590 a-f.
34 From the records of the Production and Marketing Administration, U. S. Department of Agriculture.

grants in Louisiana, for instance, flood control was one of the conditions of landholding. During the middle nineteenth century, Mississippi Valley states began to establish levee districts and to provide continuity in levee construction, but the cost was still borne by landowners.[35]

After the Civil War, the federal government made grants-in-aid to levee districts, basing such action on its power under the commerce clause to protect navigation. In 1917, Congress made its first direct appropriations for flood control and after 1927 it assumed full responsibility for flood control in the Mississippi Valley. The purchase of forest lands for flood prevention also evolved from a broadened interpretation of the commerce clause.

The climax in this development was the Tennessee Valley Act of 1934. This measure provided, along with navigation and flood control operations, a bundle of ancillary activities, such as the creation and distribution of electric power and the manufacture of fertilizer.[36] The Tennessee Valley operation has modified the structure of realty values, both rural and urban, throughout a whole region. The Tennessee Valley Act is not only a climax in constitutional interpretation, but also the highest development to date of the planning principle for the clear purpose of reorganizing land use and increasing economic opportunity. It creates a wholly new concept of governmental-private relationships, in which initiative is primarily governmental and the participation of the electorate in official decisions is extremely remote and indirect.[37] Although compliance with the Tennessee Valley Authority's programs is voluntary, the character of private activity—industrial, commercial, and personal—is inevitably shaped by the direct operations of the Authority.

[35] R. T. Ely and G. S. Wehrwein, *op. cit.*, pp. 353-59. It may be noted that along with the assumption by government (whether state or federal) of the responsibility for irrigation and flood control has come a very substantial modification of the doctrine of riparian rights. *Ibid.*, pp. 367-80.

[36] For the opinion on the constitutionality of the Act, see Ashwander et al., v. TVA, 297 U.S. 288 (1935), also United States v. Appalachian Electric Power Company, 311 U.S. 377 (1940); 48 Stat. 59 (1933) c. 32, § 2; 16 U.S.C. *et seq.*

[37] Consulting with, and even acting on the advice of, persons and local governing bodies affected by TVA decisions (see David Eli Lilienthal, *TVA: Democracy on the March,* New York, 1944) does not constitute the democratic process as ordinarily interpreted. Final decisions are the Authority's and action by it can be taken without popular approval.

THE LENGTHENING ARM OF CONTROL

As the above review indicates, government, on one claim to authority or another, will restrict the exercise of private rights in real property whenever it considers it necessary either to prevent the landowner from impinging on the rights of others, or to obtain for all, or a specially favored group of landholders, benefits presumably unattainable through private action. All forms of governmental control and assistance so far reviewed fall into one or another of these categories.

The influence of government on the use of realty has expanded from regulations to prevent fire and the collapse of buildings to far-reaching measures affecting the future of realty investment, both urban and rural. Building regulation now influences the whole technology of the construction industry; urban zoning has predetermined to a great extent the potentialities of urban realty investment; and rural zoning promises to do the same in the agricultural area. Planning programs, carrying the sanction of government, go beyond the original concepts of zoning in limiting the scope and possibilities of private investment in land. Conservation programs put government in a very influential relationship with the landowner. There are also less direct ways, to be considered later, for increasing governmental influence in a field hitherto left largely to private decision.

Because of its nature, and the degree to which its development and use is affected by public interest, a wide measure of governmental control over the uses of land is unavoidable. Certainly, without some measure of control the hazard of investment would undoubtedly be intolerable. Yet faulty or misconceived control may impede the flow of investment which is essential to economic land utilization as certainly as would the chaos of no control.[38] However, when such an impediment to the desired flow of investment does appear, government is less likely to remove the obstacle

[38] Not the least of the difficulties imposed upon investment is the diversity of regulation and the multiplicity of jurisdiction, particularly as regards urban property. Not only is there little uniformity in the building, zoning, and planning requirements of different, even neighboring, communities, but within a single community the developer of property must satisfy the requirements of and pay fees to as many as a dozen or more uncoordinated municipal agencies as well as often having to satisfy a federal finance-planning agency.

than it is to introduce new devices of regulation or stimulation, and in this way to broaden the area of intervention. Thus, the increase of governmental control introduces a new element of uncertainty in the market—uncertainty as to what government policy will be. As a result, private decisions come more and more to wait upon the judgment of public officials, and there follows a tendency for initiative to shift from the private to the public source.

CHAPTER 3

Governmental Influence on the Methods
of Real Estate Financing

THE concern of government with the establishment and protection of rights in real property gives it a natural interest in
the validity and fairness of actions that involve borrowing and
lending on the security of real estate. Moreover, being committed
to a policy of diffusion of ownership and the maintenance of small
ownerships, it is inevitable that government should make its control over financial transactions an instrument for preserving and
advancing that policy.

The process of intervention develops somewhat in this manner.
First, comes the elementary policing problem: Is the transaction
free from coercion or fraud? Next, the question of equity arises:
Are the rights and interests of borrower and lender fairly balanced?
At this stage other questions arise: In what manner may the protection granted to either party influence the flow of credit and thus
affect the state's committed objectives? Finally: What devices may
be employed to cause credit to flow in amounts and in directions
that will advance the chosen purposes? At this stage financial policy
becomes a vital instrument of land policy.

DEVELOPMENT OF MORTGAGE FINANCING

The creation of a nation of small landholders obviously involved
the extension of large amounts of credit, for settlement was a costly
process. Funds were needed to purchase land, and even after the
Homestead Act the choicest lands were rarely in the free category.
Funds were also needed to pay for improvements, tools and seed,
and to carry the settler until his land was fruitful.[1]

For these purposes the device of the mortgage loan was not only
available but had peculiar advantages. It permitted the achieve-

[1] See Clarence H. Danhof, "Farm-Making Costs and the 'Safety-Valve': 1850-1860,"
Journal of Political Economy, Vol. 49, No. 3, June 1941.

ment of ownership with a relatively low (and as events developed, a constantly lower) amount of initial cash investment, and it was largely dependent upon the security of the financed property for its repayment.

Both features were important where borrowers were likely to have little resources beyond the property itself. In addition, through successive renewals with curtail, or by regular amortization, the repayment of a mortgage loan might at least be roughly adjusted to the earning capacity of the property—a further advantage under circumstances where the property was the dominant factor in the transaction. As a consequence, mortgage financing has been synonymous with real estate financing.

The mortgage is almost as old as recorded law. For present purposes, however, its ancestry need be traced no further than from the end of the sixteenth century. By that time, the legal background of the mortgage as we know it had been well laid and many of its early crudities had been eliminated. The equity of redemption [2] had been established, and a procedure for foreclosure devised. As a distinction grew up between legal and equitable rights, title was still held by the mortgagee during the existence of the debt, but actual possession of the premises was generally left in the mortgagor, and an agreed interest payment supplanted the surrender of the yield of the property.[3]

Because of the predominance of a well-established landed interest (proverbially a debtor interest) with its passion for stability and continuity, the development of the mortgage during the next century was mainly toward the greater protection of the equity holder. Obstacles were put in the way of foreclosure, making it costly and time-consuming; and the rights of the mortgagee in possession were more and more strictly limited. Though the balance of legal opinion favored the borrower, the law in many ways was vague, leaving both parties in some uncertainty as to their rights.[4] The need for mortgage credit in those precommercial days

2 *Equity of redemption* is the right of the mortgagor to satisfy the debt and redeem the property after the date upon which the debt has become due. The time during which this right may be exercised is called the *redemption period.*

3 H. W. Chaplin, "The Story of Mortgage Law," *Harvard Law Review,* Vol. 4, 1890-91, pp. 1-14; Charles A. Keigwin, *Cases on Mortgages With Summaries of Doctrine* (Rochester, New York, 1936).

4 Robert H. Skilton, *Government and the Mortgage Debtor* (Philadelphia, 1944) p. 10.

may not have been great; certainly its expansion was not given official encouragement.

On importation to this continent, mortgage practice faced different conditions. Credit was no longer merely incidental to land ownership—it was the very essence of land acquisition and development. And the settler's need for credit often outweighed his anxiety for protection as a debtor. What the settler wanted was ample funds at a favorable interest rate, and he was willing to chance his ability to handle his part of the bargain. The availability of cheap land on an ever-broadening frontier was, at least in theory, a hedge against disaster not present in England.

In rewriting mortgage law in the colonies, the policy was clearly to induce a flow of credit. More of practice was put into statutory form and less was left to custom, thus removing much of the uncertainty as to rights and duties under the agreement. Foreclosure procedures were simplified and redemption periods were shortened, or, in some cases, eliminated altogether. At the same time, the right of the mortgagor to remain in possession before default was firmly established, and frequently this right extended to the redemption period. With these rights acknowledged, the concept of the mortgage as a lien gradually, and almost wholly, displaced that of the mortgage as a conveyance.[5]

Though the interests of the borrower were not altogether neglected, the balance of benefit was shifted to the lender. The high point in this trend was the contracts clause of the federal Constitution, which asserted the inviolability of contracts. From the available evidence, it seems clear that the provision was designed to prevent debtor relief, and particularly the relief of delinquent mortgagors, through a forced modification of contract terms such as, at times, had been imposed by colonial and state legislatures.[6]

As communities were settled, however, and open land became more difficult to acquire, a shift toward more definite solicitude for the borrower's fate became evident. This was particularly true in the new states where, as a result of national policies, small land holdings were predominant. It was less true of the older states,

[5] Ibid., p. 11.
[6] Ibid., pp. 55 ff. Also Edward S. Corwin, The Constitution and What It Means Today (Princeton, 1940) pp. 73-74; Charles A. Beard, An Economic Interpretation of the Constitution of the United States (New York, 1935) pp. 178-83.

where agriculture had declined in importance, or where large holdings under the plantation system were characteristic.

Thus, in spite of some counter swings in times of prosperity, the trend in the new agricultural states by the middle of the last century was toward the provision of long periods of redemption following foreclosure. At the present time, twenty-seven states, either by legislative or court practice, allow redemption periods of six months to two years.[7] It is interesting that all of these states were created after the establishment of the Republic and, with the exception of Alabama and Arkansas, are states in which the plantation system was never widely introduced.

UNCERTAINTY OF THE MORTGAGE CONTRACT

The policy of granting increased protection to the mortgagor went beyond merely writing the original contract terms in the mortgagor's favor. It modified the effect of the contract when in times of general distress the mortgagor's interest seemed to require it. Twenty years after the ratification of the Constitution, legislative attempts were made to circumvent the guaranteed sanctity of contracts, and each succeeding depression brought forth new methods for providing debtor relief. To this movement the federal government itself made a contribution by acting to relieve defaulting purchasers of public lands. During the sixteen years prior to 1820, eleven separate relief laws were enacted to extend or modify payments on public land contracts.[8] With the panic of 1819, the states themselves began to devise means of protecting debtors, particularly those indebted under mortgage.

Many devices were invented over the next sixty years to avoid the constitutional interdiction against statutory modification of

[7] Alabama, Arkansas, Arizona, California, Colorado, Idaho, Illinois, Indiana, Iowa, Kansas, Kentucky, Michigan, Minnesota, Missouri, Montana, Nebraska, Nevada, New Mexico, North Dakota, Oklahoma, Oregon, South Dakota, Tennessee, Utah, Washington, Wisconsin, and Wyoming. R. H. Skilton, op. cit., pp. 19-24; David A. Bridewell, "The Effects of Defective Mortgage Laws on Home Financing," Law and Contemporary Problems, Vol. 5, No. 4 (Autumn, 1938) pp. 547-48; Leonard A. Jones, A Treatise on the Law of Mortgage of Real Property (Indianapolis, 1944).

[8] Benjamin H. Hibbard, A History of the Public Land Policies (New York, 1924) pp. 92 ff. Even these moves did not prevent wholesale defaults, "when the panic came in 1819, payments due to the government for public land were in arrears many millions, most of which never were and never would be paid." See also Samuel Eliot Morison and Henry Steele Commager, The Growth of the American Republic (New York, 1937), Vol. 1, p. 338.

contractual obligations. According to Robert Skilton: [9] "The strategy usually adopted was to operate merely upon a creditor's legal remedies. The legislation was ingenious and varied. Some statutes closed the courts to contract suits for a definite or an indefinite period. Some delayed a phase of the suit, such as trial, judgment, or execution. Some created or extended the statutory right of redemption after judicial sale. Some required valuation of property before sale, and forbade sale below a certain percentage of appraised value (at least until a stipulated time had elapsed). Some created or enlarged debtors' property exemptions. All of the law purported to apply to suits on pre-existent contracts."

Judicial history has varied but, in the main, the devices were upheld,[10] although relief was generally provided only to meet a specific, current emergency, and reliance had to be placed on precedent rather than on an active statute when a new emergency arose. The mortgagee could anticipate some modification of his contract with each emergency, even though he could not foretell the precise manner and extent to which his rights would be curtailed.

The climax to this development came in the depression of the 1930's. As that crisis developed, demands for relief grew steadily more insistent. In 1932, federal authorities, and most state authorities, ordered receivers of closed banks under their respective jurisdictions to discontinue foreclosure. By the beginning of 1933, orderly court processes were interrupted in some areas. Before the suspension of banking activities in March 1933, five states had enacted mortgage moratoria. A flood of such legislation followed the bank holiday, with ten states acting during the month of

[9] R. H. Skilton, *op. cit.,* p. 60.

[10] In two decisions the Supreme Court has indicated the latitude within which debtor relief may operate. In Sturgis v. Crowninshield, 4 Wheat. 122, 200 (1819) the Court held: "The distinction between the obligation of a contract and the remedy given by the legislature to enforce that obligation has been taken at the bar, and exists in the nature of things. Without impairing the obligation of the contract, the remedy may certainly be modified as the wisdom of the nation shall direct." In Van Hoffman v. City of Quincy, 4 Wall. 535, 553-54 (1866), the language was broadened: "It is competent for the states to change the form of the remedy or to modify it otherwise, as they may see fit provided no substantial right secured by the contract is thereby impaired." Quoted in J. Douglas Poteat, "State Legislative Relief for the Mortgage Debtor During the Depression," *Law and Contemporary Problems*, Vol. 5, No. 4 (Autumn, 1938) p. 519. The temporary nature of the relief granted by the statutes is an important consideration. "Indeed," says Poteat, *ibid.,* p. 521, "it is precisely this feature on which their constitutionality depends." This criterion is established in Home Building and Loan Association v. Blaisdell, 290 U. S. 398 (1934).

March. During the remainder of 1933 and in 1934, twelve additional states enacted moratoria, making twenty-seven in all.[11]

On the whole, this legislation went much further in its effort to protect and salvage the mortgagor than any previous enactments. In most cases farm and residential property was covered irrespective of its homestead character and in some states benefits were given to corporate owners as well as to individuals. In some states the owners of commercial property, as well as of farm and residential property, obtained protection.[12]

The usual effect of the moratoria was to prohibit or impede foreclosure during the applicable period of the acts. Sometimes interest and taxes had to be paid, but in many instances payments of a fair rent on the property (which might be less than interest charges) were permitted in lieu of interest. A few of the states offered relief to all defaulting mortgagors irrespective of the nature of, or reason for, default, but more commonly a wide range of judicial discretion was permitted. The actual extent of relief granted, and the reasons for which relief was extended varied, therefore, not only from state to state but from court to court. Originally, the moratoria applied only to pre-existent contracts, but in several instances subsequent mortgages were also made subject to their provisions.[13] Questions of constitutionality arose but they were usually dealt with on the principle that the *status quo* might be maintained where an emergency prevailed and where the creditor continued to receive proper compensation.[14]

Moratoria were repeatedly extended during the decade but, with the assumption by federal agencies of a large part of the mortgage debt on farms and homes, and the gradual return of more prosperous conditions, the pressure for continued relief subsided. By the beginning of World War II, they were for all practical purposes abandoned except in New York State, where the moratorium (modified to require a 1 percent annual payment on principal) was still in force in 1947.[15]

[11] R. H. Skilton, *op. cit.,* pp. 73-78.
[12] *Ibid.,* Chapter 5.
[13] *Ibid.,* Chapter 6.
[14] *Ibid.,* Chapter 6; E. S. Corwin, *op. cit.,* p. 74; J. D. Poteat, *op. cit.,* pp. 520-25. The term "proper" was liberally interpreted from the mortgagor's point of view.
[15] Under the amended moratorium law of 1941 (Laws of New York, 1941, c. 782). See R. H. Skilton, *op. cit.,* p. 94, and *Journal of Housing,* March 1947, p. 66.

Abandonment, however, generally came through the gradual process of limiting the nature of the remedy and the classes of properties considered, rather than by outright repeal. Louisiana is probably the only state where a clear-cut repeal was enacted.[16] The aftermath was more than a mere retention of partial remedies. So widespread was the practice of granting relief from the rigidity of the mortgage contract that it may be said to have become embodied in legal usage, to be invoked with little debate whenever a new need for it might arise. In Iowa, at least, the issue has been squarely faced with a permanent statute, under which a mortgagor is entitled to petition the court for relief from foreclosure where default occurs by reason of crop failure due to climatic conditions or infestation of pests, "or when the Governor of Iowa by reason of a depression shall have by proclamation declared a state of emergency to exist in this state." [17]

State legislatures were not alone in their intervention in the mortgagor-mortgagee relationship. As early as 1931, in the last days of the Hoover Administration, an effort was made to relieve mortgage debtors through the invocation of the bankruptcy law.[18] This first attempt proved on the whole to be ineffectual. Further amendments, under the second Frazier-Lemke Act of 1935 [19] and the Chandler Act of 1938,[20] provided the means for eliminating the priority of the mortgage lien and for placing mortgage obligations in approximately the same standing as other obligations in bankruptcy proceedings. These changes in the bankruptcy statute were particularly effective in dealing with farm mortgage debt and with urban mortgage bond issues.[21] By successive extensions the Frazier-Lemke Act was kept in force until 1949.[22]

After the United States entered the war, a new type of moratorium came into existence with the passage of amendments (Octo-

16 Louisiana General Statutes Annotated (Dart Supplement 1942) §§ 5002.14-.29; R. H. Skilton, *op. cit.,* p. 94.

17 Iowa Code (Reichmann, 1939) § 12383.3, quoted in R. H. Skilton, *op. cit.,* p. 95.

18 47 Stat. 1467 (1933); 11 U.S.C. § 201 *et seq.*

19 49 Stat. 943 (1935); 11 U.S.C. § 203 (s).

20 52 Stat. 840 (1938); 11 U.S.C. § 201 *et seq.*

21 R. H. Skilton, *op. cit.,* pp. 137-44.

22 62 Stat. 198 (1948) provided extension to March 1, 1949. Although bills for the extension of these provisions beyond March 1, 1949 were pending at the close of the 1st Session, 81st Congress, no action had been taken. At least temporarily, therefore, the Frazier-Lemke statute was allowed to lapse.

ber 1942) to the Soldiers' and Sailors' Civil Relief Act of 1940.[23] This federal statute barred creditors from exercising their remedies during the period of the borrower's military service.

DECLINE OF THE DEFICIENCY JUDGMENT

The moratorium met only one phase of the defaulted debtor's problem. It gave him time in which to repair his fortunes, or to negotiate for modified terms with his creditor, but it could not lighten his personal liability under a deficiency judgment.

American mortgage laws in most states make two significant departures from English foreclosure practice. In England, the mortgagee may obtain title by taking and holding possession beyond the limitation on the right of redemption, or by proceeding to obtain title under strict foreclosure.[24] If either course is adopted the debt is considered to be discharged and all claims canceled. Or, a public sale, in which the mortgagee may not participate, may be required by court decree. In the latter case, the mortgagee may lay claim on the debtor for any deficiency in the amount received from sale. In this country, the method of obtaining title has generally been limited to public sale under the jurisdiction of the court, although the mortgagee is permitted to bid at the sale and at the same time to retain his right to sue for a deficiency judgment.[25]

The first departure—the requirement of sale—by avoiding the possibility that the creditor might obtain property greater in value than the amount of the debt was undoubtedly taken in the mortgagor's interest. But the second—permitting the mortgagee to bid and, at the same time, to sue on the covenant—was clearly in the lender's interest. Particularly in times of distress, when values were low and purchasers few, nominal bidding by a mortgagee might, and often did, leave the mortgagor with a burden from which there was no escape but bankruptcy.[26]

In the course of a century, various means were used to escape

---

23 54 Stat. 1179 (1940), as amended by 56 Stat. 769 (1942).

24 Strict foreclosure "is an action in which a decree is rendered barring the mortgagor's equity, and vesting the absolute estate in the mortgagee, if the debt is not paid within a certain time after the rendition of the decree." Christopher Gustavus Tiedeman, *The American Law of Real Property* (St. Louis, 1924) p. 272.

25 R. H. Skilton, *op. cit.*, pp. 11-12, 116-17.

26 D. A. Bridewell, *op. cit.*, p. 558.

this contingency. Sometimes a substantial minimum limit was put on the amount of the price bid at a foreclosure sale. Another method was to permit redemption at the amount of the sales price (plus interest and costs). But the real drive on the deficiency judgment came with the depression of the 1930's. The approach usually was to prevent nominal bidding by postponing sales, by establishing minimum sales prices, by relating the deficiency to an appraisal of "fair value" rather than sales price, and limiting the time during which an appraisal might be sought and a suit be brought, or by limiting the time within which a judgment could be enforced. In seven states the effect of the statutes is to eliminate the possibility of a deficiency judgment.[27]

Unlike the state moratorium laws, deficiency judgment legislation has generally been applicable to the future as well as to the past, and consequently results in a permanent modification in mortgage procedure. Difficulties with constitutionality seem on the whole to have been overcome.[28]

SHORTCOMINGS OF THE MORTGAGE DEVICE

In spite of its apparent adaptability to the requirements of realty finance, the mortgage has revealed serious weaknesses in its adaptability to the requirements of a fluid, expanding society. A number of these weaknesses resulted from practices which, due either to legal requirements or to custom, became characteristic of the mortgage lending system; others are more deeply imbedded in the mortgage device itself.

Of the first class of weaknesses, Horace Russell lists eight, which he considers to have been major contributors to the debacle of the thirties (and which, indeed, were present in all previous disasters): "First was the general use of short-term mortgage loans, which had to be refinanced every few years with high commissions and financing charges. Second was the general practice of lending only a small amount on the security of the first mortgage, which necessitated junior financing with all the hazards to the borrower which that practice involved. Third was the general use of lump-sum rather than amortized mortgages, which necessitated the borrower repaying the entire amount of the mortgage at one time or refinanc-

27 Arizona, Arkansas, California, Louisiana, Montana, Nebraska, South Dakota.
28 R. H. Skilton, op. cit., pp. 121-34; J. D. Poteat, op. cit., pp. 529-36.

ing it. Fourth was the prevailing high interest rates generally charged on all such mortgage loans in contradistinction to the low interest rates charged on railroad, public utility, and other types of long-term loans. Fifth was the absence of a steady market for mortgages as a preferred type of investment, due to the lack of facilities for insuring the repayment of mortgage loans and to the lack of a sufficient number of sound mortgage associations operating on a national basis, which would create a market for this type of investment. Sixth was the lack of any credit facilities for home-financing institutions from which such institutions could borrow in order to meet reasonable withdrawal requests of their investors during times of emergency and to meet the usual requirements of their borrowers. Seventh was the lack of any insurance facilities whereby shareholders and depositors in home-financing institutions might be assured of the repayment of their invested funds. Eighth was the absence of proper lending and appraisal practices and procedure and the impossibility of obtaining uniform, cooperative action among thousands of widely scattered local home-financing institutions." [29]

Many of these reputed defects have, in part at least, been remedied by legislation to be discussed below. Many, however, persist because of the unsolved problems arising from the variety, rigidity, cumbrousness, and costliness of mortgage procedures. As is true with all the substantive law of real property, mortgage law lies in the province of the states; and the states have well expressed their separate sovereignties in the variety of their legislation. Diversity in the proffered remedies and the stipulated procedure impedes the flow of funds on a national basis and tends to maintain localism in mortgage lending. Efforts at uniform mortgage legislation (corresponding to the universally adopted Negotiable Instruments Act) have so far borne little fruit.

The rigidity of the mortgage contract creates another deterrent to the flow of funds. The now general practice of regularly amortizing mortgage loans is at best only a partial remedy. It does prevent the hazard of large payments to be made under uncertain future conditions, and it does, very roughly, reduce the outstanding

[29] Horace Russell, "Private Housing Legal Problems," *Housing, the Continuing Problem* (National Resources Planning Board, Washington, December 1940) pp. 41-42.

obligation in some relationship with the probable ultimate decline in the value of the security. But the amortization arrangements are themselves usually fixed and inflexible and, if combined with interest in one payment of constant amount, they prevent (except by special arrangement with the lender) any adjustment to a varying rental or personal income. Moreover, the dangers of inflexibility are increased with the reduction of down payments and the extension of the repayment period.[30]

In contrast to the ordinary collateral loan of commercial banking, the mortgage contract does not (perhaps for good reason) provide either for increasing the amount of security or for quickly calling the loan in a period of falling value. Consequently, mortgage lending practice commonly requires that the amount loaned be limited to a figure considered to be not more than the lowest value to which the security may fall during the term of the loan. The decline in the availability of the deficiency judgment emphasizes the importance of this principle. Yet, as we shall find, the exercise of the principle runs counter to a public policy that seeks to liberalize lending terms, irrespective of the peculiar characteristics of the transaction.

The slowness and costliness of the foreclosure procedures which the mortgagee must follow in most states, even when unimpeded by a moratorium, are notorious.[31] These procedures add to the initial charges and cost of money to the borrower, and they add to the risk of the lender. They tend to reduce the relative availability of mortgage funds in states where foreclosure procedures are the most onerous, and they particularly increase the cost of hazard on loans of small amounts. These conditions have often made it difficult for private institutions to comply with an expansionist credit policy and consequently have evoked measures to compensate for the impediments introduced by state law. Indeed, the later history

30 Recently, some institutions have adopted the practice of writing into the mortgage loan agreement conditions under which the amortization payment might be modified to meet temporary hardship on the part of the borrower. This practice, however, appears not to be widespread. Effort has also been made to include such provisions in Federal Housing Administration procedure.

31 H. Russell, *op. cit.*, pp. 45-52; D. A. Bridewell, *op. cit.*, pp. 549-58. In this connection it may be noted that long redemption periods, characteristic of farm mortgage credits, become particularly burdensome and hazardous to the lender on urban property.

of federal intervention is concerned in large part with efforts in this direction.

In addition to the problems just discussed, two special questions arise concerning the adaptability of the mortgage device to current real estate and construction requirements. These questions center on "fixtures" and construction loans.

THE PROBLEM OF "FIXTURES"

The distinction between movable and real property, while never wholly clear, was in early times usually not difficult to draw. What was fixed to the land was a "fixture" and thus part of the real estate and eligible as security for a real estate mortgage loan. In the course of time, however, many fixtures have become less fixed; new elements of uncertain status have been added to the structure; and the structure itself in some respects has become less definite in its affixation. Electrical equipment (such as ranges, refrigerators, laundry machines, and ventilating fans) which is affixed only by a plug-in device, certain easily-removed gas-fired equipment, certain classes of furniture, partially affixed (such as folding beds and removable partitions)—these are only a few in a long list of questionable items. With the increasing use of prefabricated building methods, the list may be greatly extended.

The traditional tests for determining whether or not an article is a fixture are the following: (1) the manner of its annexation to the land or to the structure; (2) its adaptability to the use and purpose for which the realty is used, or its essentiality to the realization of that use; (3) the intention of the parties making the annexation; and (4) the specific agreement as between buyer and seller, landlord and tenant, mortgagor and mortgagee as to what is, or is not, real estate.[32]

With an increase in the number of disputable items, tests (2), (3), and (4) have become more important. State law, however, varies widely on this point and custom and court decisions within states have added to the range of variation. The wide use of conditional sales contracts, and of chattel mortgages, complicates the situation by introducing additional parties into the process of acquiring a complete and usable property.

[32] C. G. Tiedeman, *op. cit.*, Chapter 2; L. A. Jones, *op. cit.*, Vol. 1, Chapter 11.

The mortgagee has several problems because of this situation. On foreclosure, he may find the security stripped and unusable without additional expense. Legal definitions may prevent his blanketing certain items under the mortgage to the detriment of his security and of his ability to include their value in estimating the legal limit of the loan. Finally, the extensive use of instalment credit for financing equipment that cannot be classed as real property may seriously affect the mortgagor's ability to carry the total debt.

Therefore, the problem relates not only to the precautions necessary for the protection of the security but to the ability of the lender to offer a financing device that will economically and completely meet the borrower's requirements. Recent modifications providing for a more flexible definition of fixtures have been made in many state laws, and, though custom may lag in some jurisdictions, these changes do demonstrate the adaptability of mortgage law to new conditions.[33]

THE PROBLEM OF CONSTRUCTION LOANS

The adaptability of law and custom to modern requirements appears less satisfactory in the case of construction loans. The mortgage, according to its original conception, is a conveyance of, or a lien on, an existing property—land, or land with structures on it. The purpose to which the proceeds of a mortgage loan are put—purchase, debt refunding, or personal convenience—plays no part in the legal concepts involved. One of the important needs for credit, however, is for development and construction. In this case, the basis of the loan is not the value of existing real property but a value that will exist only when the proposed improvements have been completed. In this case the success of the loan transaction will be determined by a number of conditions, each of which can be estimated only roughly at the time the terms of credit are agreed upon. These conditions are the eventual utility and earning power of the improvements, the probability of completion within an estimated limit of cost, the likelihood of substitution of long-term

[33] Another evidence of adaptability is the apparently increasing popularity of the so-called "open-end" mortgage, which permits successive loans to be made with the same instrument for the purpose of financing structural repairs, replacing or adding equipment, etc. See *Fortune Magazine*, Vol. 40, No. 3 (September 1949) p. 18.

financing on completion, and the ability of the borrower to carry out his commitments.

Despite these differences between developmental and long-term real estate finance, the mortgage loan, characteristically designed for the latter, is also the principal medium for the former. Two methods are generally followed: (1) a single loan agreement may be made, with amounts disbursed during the developmental period until, at completion, the entire amount has been advanced; or (2) two agreements may be entered into, usually with separate lenders, one of whom provides the entire amount of the loan on the completion of the improvements and the other, limited to the construction period, advances funds as the work proceeds. In both instances, however, the mortgage instrument is ordinarily used. The property, as it exists and as it is to be, provides the security for the loan.

Historically, the owner (or purchaser) of the property rather than the builder or developer arranged the financing, usually through a pledge of the property, and he made progress payments to the builder. The builder, therefore, needed only to carry himself from payment to payment, either out of his own resources or with the proceeds of a short-term bank loan. This system permitted builders to operate with little or no capital and gave rise to an industry unusually lacking in internal financial resources.

Arrangements of this kind have prevailed in spite of the growing importance of the merchant builder who constructs houses for future sale. Such a builder is essentially a manufacturer producing for a market rather than for specific, precontracted purchasers and he has financial requirements similar to those of other producers. For this type of operation, mortgage financing is often especially cumbersome, restrictive, and costly. The land may be covered with a blanket mortgage subject to release clauses; a number of lots may be released under a new mortgage contract to provide funds for construction; a third transaction providing funds for the individual purchaser is necessary on sale of the completed house. Each of these transactions involves negotiation, delay, title search, and expense characteristic of no other form of business finance.

Another method is to arrange separate mortgages on the prospective dwellings, to obtain advances on each mortgage as the work proceeds, and to assign each mortgage, or substitute another, on completion and sale of the property. This method, while simpler in some ways, is still exceedingly clumsy and is ill-adapted to a mass operation. Moreover, the lender, being skeptical of the market and even more skeptical of the borrower's capacity to repay, except on a basis of quick sale, is disinclined to extend credit except for a small number of units. In a few centers the merchant builder, on the basis of commitments from a mortgage lending institution to make mortgage loans on completion and sale of property, can obtain a bank loan to finance construction. This practice is generally less complex and less costly than the other procedures outlined, but it appears to be not widely employed.

Whatever the method used, the finished product is a paramount consideration in the transaction. The situation is much as if, in automobile manufacture, each car, or group of cars, either had been sold to individual purchasers or had purchaser-financing provided for before the first item had been placed on the assembly line. Such a fusion of producer and consumer credit would be an impossibility in the mass production industries. It is undoubtedly one of the influences retarding the industrialization of house-building.

The situation has become even more crucial with the development of factory fabrication, in which the bulk of the structure may be produced apart from the land. As the prefabricating industry was evolving before World War II, production was in large part limited by orders in hand. Dealers were required to pay cash on delivery, and orders were usually not placed until the purchaser was found and his financing arranged, thus making production contingent on the flow of credit to the consumer.

The difficulties discussed above have led to a number of interventionary steps: the granting of "firm commitments" [34] to builders by the Federal Housing Administration; the insurance, by that same agency, of construction advances on rental housing mortgages and on mortgages securing single family houses with clauses permitting release of separate parcels upon sale; the provision of direct government loans to manufacturers of prefabricated houses to meet interim working capital requirements; the insurance of loans by FHA for the same purpose.[35] Some of these actions have had con-

[34] Agreements entered into prior to construction to insure loans on completion, with the builder as mortgagor, irrespective of the builder evidencing sales contracts.
[35] See Chapters 6 and 7.

siderable success, others have failed and been abandoned, still others proceed in an experimental fashion. But the problem remains.

OTHER METHODS OF REALTY FINANCE

The typical mortgage loan is, and has been, made by a single lender. Prior to the 1930's, mortgage participations under a trust agreement (often accompanied by a guarantee of payment) were common, and, along with the real estate mortgage bond issue, had a great but ephemeral vogue in the financing of apartment houses, office buildings, and hotels. Discredited by abuses, later made impracticable by securities regulations, and rendered at least temporarily unnecessary by the recent abundance of institutional mortgage funds, mortgage participation and bond issues have never been revived for private operations.[36]

In a few of the states, ground rents, long-term leases, and land-trust certificates have served as important auxiliary devices in financing the improvement of real property.[37] But the general desire for fee ownership, combined with the widespread disfavor in which leasehold mortgages are held by state laws regulating institutional investment, has prevented any important extension of the ground rent system.

The financing device most commonly used as an alternative to the mortgage loan is the land contract, or contract for deed. Under this instrument, the buyer is granted possession but is not given title until the conditions of the contract are fulfilled. Upon default, repossession may be obtained by the vendor, at least theoretically, without recourse to foreclosure.[38] Probably the greatest use of land

36 Louis S. Posner, "The Lesson of Guaranteed Mortgage Certificates," *Harvard Business Review*, Vol. 21, No. 5 (September 1948).

For further treatment of this subject, see Ernest M. Fisher, *Urban Real Estate Markets and Their Financing Needs* (National Bureau of Economic Research, Financial Research Program, mimeo. 1950) Chapter 2. Housing properties owned by municipal housing authorities have recently been financed by bond issues. The possibility also exists legally of financing real estate operations by the issuance to a lending institution, or institutions, of bonds secured by all the assets of the developing corporation. A mortgage may be involved but it will not be the sole consideration in making the loan. Financing of this type is not limited by the loan-to-value ratio of the customary mortgage loan, but, as with other bond financing, rests almost wholly on the discretion of the lender.

37 R. H. Skilton, *op. cit.*, p. 36. E. M. Fisher, *op. cit.*, Chapter 2.

38 Herbert Thorndike Tiffany, *A Treatise on the Modern Law of Real Property* (new abridged ed., Chicago, 1940) p. 1024.

contracts in this country was in connection with the sale of public
lands. Under the federal system, the entryman was required to
make a partial payment on obtaining possession, and to pay the
remainder in annual instalments.[39] Failure to make a payment resulted in the forfeiture of all previous payments, as well as of
improvements made by the settler. Nothing like an equity of redemption was recognized, although the relief acts, particularly
those passed from 1821 to 1832, in effect provided a period of
redemption by extending the payment period. For practical purposes, this device recognized an equitable right of the settler in the
land for which he had contracted.[40]

In later years, the land contract has been extensively used in
the sale of urban lots and houses, especially where the initial cash
payment was less than necessary to permit financing by a conventional mortgage loan. In this case the land contract might be the
sole financial device, or a device supplemental to a mortgage loan.
In many jurisdictions, the courts have considered the buyer under
a land contract as having an equitable interest in the property to
the extent of his payments or improvements and have consequently
granted the right of redemption after default.[41] Where this has
occurred, the distinction between the contract and the mortgage
is largely erased, and the advantage to the lender or vendor of
unimpeded repossession after default is lost. Because of this, and
because of the increasing availability of mortgage funds on a high
ratio of loan to value, the land contract has declined in popularity
since the twenties.

The use of equity funds in the form of stock or trust participations has been of relatively minor importance in realty finance. A
serious effort to substitute these methods of finance for debt financing was made in connection with cooperative apartments during
the building boom of the twenties, and on commercial structures

[39] The law of 1796 provided for final payment at the end of one year. The law of
1800 extended the payment period to four years. The public credit system was
abandoned in 1820, all subsequent sales being financed by cash or private loan.
B. H. Hibbard, *op. cit.,* pp. 82, 83, and 94.

[40] *Ibid.,* pp. 95-96.

[41] H. T. Tiffany, *op. cit.,* pp. 1024-25. Land contracts appear also to have been
frequently used by insurance companies and banks, particularly mutual savings
banks, in selling foreclosed properties.

late in that era, as mortgage funds began to be less plentiful.[42] Even in these instances, it was rare indeed that the substitution was so complete as to eliminate the need for mortgage loans.

Recently, financing through the direct acquisition of income property by financial institutions has grown into a promise of importance, but the weight of governmental policy has been on the side of discouragement rather than incentive to equity investment. Corporate income taxes, for instance, produce both a deterrent to equity investment and an inducement to debt financing in real estate corporations. The property tax often produces a risk that is likely to give pause to the most venturesome investor.[43] At the same time, the reduction of mortgage interest rates and the increase in loan-to-value ratios and aggressive competition among mortgage lenders have reduced alike the need and the incentive to invest venture funds. On the whole, the dependence of real estate financing on the mortgage instrument is today probably greater than at any time in history and is so largely as the outgrowth of governmental influences.

AREAS OF CONFLICT

Glancing back over the course of governmental policy, a number of conflicts and inconsistencies are evident. There have been, and still remain, serious conflicts between state and federal viewpoints, inconsistencies among the laws of the states and between an expansionist federal policy on the one hand and a cumbersome financial instrument on the other. Perhaps the most far-reaching area of conflict develops from the effort made, since the early days of the Republic, to increase the protection of the borrower under a mortgage agreement and at the same time to satisfy increasing demands for more extensive and more liberal credit.

Despite endeavors to meet these problems, the rigidity of the mortgage contract and the variety, slowness, and costliness of mortgage procedures have on the whole been allowed to remain. Taking into account the depreciability of the security over the customarily long period of loan repayment, the possibility that the security may

[42] Miles L. Colean, *American Housing* (The Twentieth Century Fund, New York, 1944) pp. 233-34.
[43] See Chapter 9, for a more extended discussion of the effects of tax policy on equity investment.

be willfully destroyed before the lender's eyes but beyond his control, and the increasing dubiety of his recourse to deficiency judgments, the characteristics of the mortgage tend to make it relatively unattractive, from the lender's point of view. The natural reaction is to temper the availability of mortgage funds at times when a choice of investment outlets is present and to stiffen the terms of mortgage loans by comparison with other types of borrowing. The difficulties of creating a consistent and equitable policy are tremendous. At the same time we may note the intrusion of a new complication.

Throughout financial history, the basis for extending credit has been the prospect of repayment. The greater the resources of the borrower, the better the terms he might exact from the lender. Where, however, the transaction is made an instrument of public policy, the strict application of this principle meets with difficulties. If, for instance, it is determined to have a nation of individual landholders, the question arises whether the ability to pay can be the sole, or even the compelling, criterion. In the pursuance of such a policy it may be considered desirable to extend credit to persons who can pay very little, and who consequently require credit on such generous terms as to create risks beyond the limits of both prudent lending practice and supervisory policy. The requirements for credit, from this point of view, may be in an exactly reverse ratio to the borrower's resources.[44]

The individual states have never been able to clear the areas of conflict between a rigid financial instrument and a variable economic situation, between the need for borrowed funds and the ability to repay, and between expanded demands for funds and restrictions that reduce the volume of funds. In fact, by the trend of their relief legislation and the future uncertainty engendered by it, the states have undoubtedly aggravated the conflicts. They have, moreover, created an additional complexity by the variety of the courses they have followed, so that confusion has been added to inconsistency. The high interest rates on real estate loans, and particularly on farm loans, that were prevalent (especially in the southern and western states) prior to the era of federal intervention offered evidence that debtor relief did not in the long run contribute to a sound or an adequate mortgage credit system.

[44] See Chapter 5 for further discussion of this question.

The multiplicity of jurisdictions plainly offered difficulties to the formulation and advancement of a national real estate credit policy. While public land was plentiful, the influence of the federal government was fairly direct, since it was at least in a position to offer new land to those dispossessed of their property. Because, however, the central government lacked power to touch the substantive law of real property, the federal influence became increasingly remote as the land passed from its control.

Yet, having encouraged the creation of small ownerships through every available means, the federal government, after the post-Civil War disillusionment, was certain to be subjected to pressure from the recipients of free land for protection against the calamities to which the great expansion of cultivation and credit had subjected them. Nevertheless, this movement was surprisingly slow in developing. The populist agitation of the eighties and nineties, for instance, was only slightly concerned with the credit system; and its efforts to invoke the federal power were directed at freight and warehouse rate legislation and general monetary legislation rather than specifically toward mortgage credit.[45]

By the 1930's, however, faith both in the necessity for, and the efficacy of, federal intervention had vastly increased. By that time the federal government had already moved far into the field of credit control through the Federal Reserve System and the Land Bank System. Against the growth of federal power, the ability of the states to provide relief seemed slow, piecemeal, and insufficient. General opinion accepted the premises that the underlying weaknesses of the realty economy were beyond the capacity of the states to correct, and that relief on the scale demanded by the times and the restoration of a flow of credit required to meet future needs must come mainly from the federal authority.

The condition of urban real estate in the late twenties was no less precarious than that of farmland. As farm values were swollen by confidence in foreign markets, so urban values had been inflated by a belief in endless city growth. In both areas, credit had been expanded, equities had been stretched thin, and, in its diffusion, ownership had in many instances been weakened. With the collapse, the demands upon the federal government became irresistible.

[45] S. E. Morison and H. S. Commager, *op. cit.*, Vol. 2, pp. 119, 211, 241-65, and 435.

Subsequent federal intervention took five main directions: (1) a series of broad economic measures involving heavy federal expenditure designed to restore and maintain the farm economy and hence farm values; (2) the use of federal credit and subsidies to halt rural and urban foreclosures and to salvage ownerships; (3) the creation of new mortgage credit institutions, usually supported by government capital, and sometimes resulting in a wholly governmental operation; (4) the creation of a number of devices for restoring public confidence in private credit institutions and for renewing and expanding their lending activity; and (5) the direct use of federal funds for the alleviation of urban tenancy and the expansion of farm ownership.

Through these actions the federal government was able to halt liquidation by a wholesale assumption of private contracts, revising them as necessary to meet the realities of the situation. It then moved to commit its own funds, to encourage lenders to make commitments in a falling and disordered market, and to permit purchasers to borrow without loss of liquidity. The specific means chosen will be discussed below. Here it need only be noted that the national land policy created a credit problem that strained the capacity of traditional devices and methods. In the end, the federal government, which had laid down the policy, was called upon to salvage and restore what it had created.

Governmental Regulation of Institutions

Financing Real Estate

THE state has concerned itself with financial institutions for two reasons: to assure adequate credit facilities and to safeguard invested savings. These separate interests, however, are often contradictory, one aim being dynamic and, to a degree, speculative, while the other is conservatory. From the one side government stimulates while from the other it restrains; and out of the shifting balance between these two ends the determination of a credit policy is attempted.

Since this is a study of the relation of government to real estate finance, we are interested only in the influence of government on institutions financing real estate, and only to the extent that government influences the real estate financial policies of these institutions. Yet nearly all financial institutions are engaged to some extent in mortgage lending, specialization in real estate finance being a minor feature of the financial system and of comparatively recent importance. The coverage of the chapter must, therefore, be broad.

GROWTH OF PRIVATE CREDIT INSTITUTIONS

A nation committed to a policy of widespread diffusion of real property ownership might be expected early to have devised credit institutions especially suited to meet the long-term credit requirements of such an objective. Actually, however, federal land policy during the years of expansion was unaccompanied by a land credit policy.[1] The extensive needs for credit to finance land settlement and improvement were supplied by individual lenders and by state and private banks. These early institutions operated without coordination, and with relatively little supervision, and were more

1 Except to the extent that time payments were permitted on the purchase of public lands prior to 1820.

often attuned to the speculative potentials of the land movement than to the requirements of credit for productive purposes.

As early as the seventeenth century, efforts were made in Massachusetts and in other New England colonies to organize private banks to make loans on the security of real estate and personal collateral; in the early years of the eighteenth century these efforts began to bear fruit.[2] In 1732 in Connecticut, and in 1740 in Massachusetts, land banks were established that issued notes on the security of real estate mortgages, but these institutions were short-lived.[3] In spite of this setback, many colonies did establish loan offices or public land banks that issued notes on the security of farm mortgages; and numerous private land bank schemes were devised, some of which were put into actual operation.[4] Inept or unscrupulous management resulted in widespread failures, bringing the whole theory of land bank finance into bad odor, a popular disfavor which benefited Hamilton in his successful effort to defeat the formation of a state land bank in New York in 1784.[5]

Nevertheless, the idea was not abandoned. The early part of the nineteenth century saw the development in the southern states of property banks, which were mainly associations of borrowers subscribing mortgages on land for capital stock and making loans from funds obtained by the sale of bonds secured by mortgages and guaranteed by the states.[6] Between 1840 and 1850 a regular farm mortgage banking business developed in the Middle West.[7] In both cases, however, the tendency to finance on the basis of anticipated land values brought widespread failures.

Mortgage lending was not limited to these specialized institutions. Individual lenders remained the principal source of credit; and, in spite of Hamilton's admonitions on the incompatibility of mortgage paper with the requirements of commercial banking,

---

2 Andrew McFarland Davis, *Provincial Banks: Land and Silver*, Publication of the Colonial Society of Massachusetts (Boston, 1900) Vol. 3, pp. 2-40; *Currency and Banking in the Province of Massachusetts Bay* (New York, 1901) Part 2; and Davis R. Dewey, *Financial History of the United States* (New York, 1931) p. 24.

3 *Ibid.*, pp. 25-26; Earl S. Sparks, *History and Theory of Agricultural Credit in the United States* (New York, 1932) pp. 53-54. The brief and stormy histories of these institutions are given in A. M. Davis, *op. cit.*, and in his *A Connecticut Land Bank of the Eighteenth Century* (Cambridge, 1898).

4 E. S. Sparks, *op. cit.*, pp. 77-78.

5 Nathan Schachner, *Alexander Hamilton* (New York, 1946) pp. 181-82.

6 E. S. Sparks, *op. cit.*, pp. 6-7 and 83.

7 *Ibid.*, p. 177.

state-chartered commercial banks, from the beginning of the Republic, were heavily involved in loans on both farm and town property.[8] Even the Second Bank of the United States, particularly through its southern and western branches, became an important holder of mortgage paper and, as events turned out, of foreclosed property.[9]

In spite of restrictions and repeated disasters, state banks continued to be important sources of mortgage credit. In their fusion of mortgage and commercial lending, little differentiation between the principles of short-term and long-term credit was made either by the banks or by the laws under which they were regulated. The mortgage was treated as an intermediate-term loan (of three to five years) rather than a true long-term loan, as was dictated by the characteristics of real estate investment.

Even in national banks, mortgage and commercial credit were blended in somewhat the same way as in state institutions. Although the original Act [10] was designed to keep national banks out of the mortgage lending field, there is strong evidence that in practice the prohibition was elastic.[11] In 1913, the Federal Reserve Act permitted national banks to make loans on farm property for five years and up to 50 percent of appraisal value (provided such loans did not, in the aggregate, exceed 25 percent of the bank's capital and surplus or one-third of its time deposits).[12] In 1916, the first direct authorization to make nonfarm loans was granted, but the contract term was limited to one year and the maximum loan-to-value ratio was set at 50 percent. A further liberalization in 1927 extended the allowable term of nonfarm mortgage loans to five years and permitted the aggregate of such loans to reach 50 percent of a bank's time deposits.[13]

[8] *Ibid.*, pp. 57-58 and 177. Also, George E. Barnett, *State Banking in the United States Since the Passage of the National Bank Act,* Johns Hopkins Studies in Historical and Political Science, Vol. 20, Nos. 2-3 (Baltimore, 1902) p. 50.

[9] E. S. Sparks, *op. cit.*, p. 270.

[10] 13 Stat. 99 (1864); 12 U.S.C. 8.

[11] Homer Hoyt, *A Hundred Years of Land Values in Chicago* (Chicago, 1933) p. 445.

[12] 38 Stat. 251 (1915); 12 U.S.C. 221.

[13] 39 Stat. 360 (1916); 12 U.S.C. 641. Amendments to the Banking Act enacted in 1935 (49 Stat. 684) are part of the effort to increase funds for mortgage lending in the midst of the depression. They permitted national banks to make ten-year loans up to 60 percent of value, provided at least 40 percent of the loan was amortized during the period. National banks at this time were also permitted to make mortgage loans insured by the Federal Housing Administration.

These measures, in combination with the generally more liberal provisions governing the operations of state banks, made mortgage lending an integral part of the commercial banking structure. This combination of function had, of course, the advantage of providing real estate with sources of credit not otherwise available. Nevertheless, it had the danger of tying realty finance to the highly variable conditions of commercial credit, thus affecting the former with the same volatility as the latter, and of placing real estate loans and commercial loans into direct competition for the same funds, a situation likely on the whole to be unfavorable to realty.

From the middle of the nineteenth century, life insurance companies became important sources of mortgage funds. Not being subject to sudden demands for liquidity as were commercial banks, life insurance companies could treat the real estate loan as a long-term, slowly liquidating investment. Furthermore, because their investments were usually less limited geographically than those of banks, they could to a greater degree make funds available in undercapitalized areas and avoid the risk of being tied to the fortunes of a single area.

These were important advantages, but they were not sufficient to bring about a complete solution of the credit requirements of real estate. In fact, at no time for which records are available have the insurance companies as a group held much more than 18 percent of the total real estate mortgage debt,[14] although in 1929 insurance companies had approximately 40 percent of their admitted assets in mortgage loans.[15]

Mutual savings banks and cooperative banks date from an earlier period, but their growth was more limited and was confined mainly to the Middle Atlantic and New England regions. While about 28 percent of savings bank investments were real estate loans in 1948, as compared with approximately 7 percent for commercial banks and about 17 percent for insurance companies,[16] their principal

[14] *Survey of Current Business,* September 1946, Table 9, p. 17.

[15] Mortgage investments of life insurance companies are from annual estimates of the Home Loan Bank Board. At the end of 1948, the proportion of mortgage loans to assets was 19.4 percent, after having dropped to as low a ratio as 14.5 percent in 1945. In spite of the much lower ratio of mortgages to total assets, the dollar volume of mortgages held had actually increased since 1929 to a record level of $10.8 billion at the end of 1948. It may be noted that if the 1929 ratio prevailed today insurance companies would hold about half the total mortgage debt.

[16] Figures for mutual savings banks and commercial banks are from the *86th*

interest, both because of the law and of managerial policy, was the encouragement and protection of thrift rather than the financing of real estate.

The first of our present-day institutions to be established for the specific purpose of meeting real estate credit needs were the savings (or building) and loan associations. From a modest, semi-philanthropic start in 1831, these associations have grown in importance until, at the end of 1948, they held 31 percent of the total residential mortgage debt on one- to four-family nonfarm houses and close to one-fifth of the total nonfarm mortgage debt.[17] During their growth, savings and loan associations have been transformed from a very simple form of cooperative society in which nearly every shareholder was a borrower to institutions in which saving need not be associated with borrowing. The word "building" has generally been displaced in their title by the word "savings," and the institutions themselves have come more and more to resemble mutual savings institutions, although their investments have continued to be predominantly in home mortgages. During the latter part of the last century, many building and loan associations operated on a national basis, both as to sources of funds and distribution of loans. The spectacular failure of the "nationals," however, led to closer supervision and greater geographical limitation of activity.[18] Today, they are characteristically local institutions depending mainly on local capital and lending within a restricted area.

To this group of institutions may be added the mortgage bond houses and mortgage guarantee companies, organized under state incorporation laws and to a minor degree subject to state regulation. They flourished mainly during the first quarter of this century, first as farm mortgage investment media and later as means of financing urban income property of all types. Their bond and certificate issues were secured either by a pool of mortgages, or, in the case of large

Annual Report of the Comptroller of the Currency 1948; for insurance companies from the annual survey of the Home Loan Bank Board. By contrast with the current situation, many savings banks during the 1920's and 1930's held 50 to 60 percent of their investments in the form of real estate loans.

17 Seymour Dexter, A Treatise on Cooperative Savings and Loan Associations (New York, 1889) p. 43; History of Building and Loan in the United States, Morton Bodfish, ed. (U. S. Building and Loan League, Chicago, 1931) pp. 57-58. Estimates of savings and loan business are based on Federal Home Loan Bank and Department of Commerce figures.

18 M. Bodfish, op. cit., Chapter 7.

urban properties, by a mortgage on a single development. During the boom years of the 1920's, the bond houses competed with the more strictly supervised financial institutions, but failures led to a decline in their importance as a source of farm credit and to their disappearance as a factor in the urban mortgage market.

Up to 1916 in the farm, and to 1932 in the urban, market the institutions described above (aside from individuals and various classes of trusts, pension funds, and nonfinancial institutions, such as universities and foundations) composed the sources of mortgage funds.[19] With the exception of the national banks, for which mortgage lending was a minor and relatively recent function, all of the institutions operated under state charter. With the exception of the building (or savings) and loan associations and the mortgage bond houses, none of the institutions providing real estate credit was established primarily for that purpose, nor have real estate loans often, or for long, received their principal attention. The incidental and optional character of most institutional mortgage lending is worthy of note because of its influence on the availability of mortgage funds and on subsequent efforts by government to increase the amount of mortgage lending.

INFLUENCE OF THE STATE ON INSTITUTIONAL POLICY

All of the institutions mentioned above are subject to some form of regulation, either by state or federal government, or both. The regulation exists by virtue of the power to charter financial institutions, the provisions of institutional charters, the general laws regulating institutional investment, and the authority granted to the supervisory agencies of government. Each type of regulation gives government important means for influencing credit policies.

Because all such regulation is a matter of state jurisdiction, excepting that of the national banks and the more recent federal institutions, there is little national uniformity. Moreover, within both federal and state spheres of influence, there is great variety among the laws affecting different types of institutions.

[19] Mention should also be made of such specialized institutions as the Investors Syndicate (Minneapolis) and Allied Building Credits (St. Paul). These institutions operate under state charter and their activity, which is national in scope, has been concerned with mortgage lending, property improvement loans, and business credits in fields of construction and materials distribution.

The result is that we have, instead of a single mortgage credit system, or a single governmental policy affecting institutional activity, a number of systems and policies. The governmental influence, while pervasive, is not uniform; and its effect on the flow of credit is mixed. Indeed, its effect on the availability of mortgage credit has often not been its most direct concern. The primary and most evident aim of governmental supervision has been to safeguard the funds placed in institutional hands. Like the regulations affecting the construction of buildings, the regulation of investment activity is the product of successive disasters, and often, either in whole or in part, has not appeared until long after the creation of the institutions themselves.[20]

CHARTERING POWER

A primary impact of the state upon the financial system comes from its power to charter financial institutions. This power, of course, is fundamental to the creation of large pools of credit and to the manner and method through which credit is made available for realty needs. Underchartering may result in an insufficiency of credit; overchartering may bring the reverse. However, there is little evidence that, prior to the 1930's, the chartering power was used with any positive intent of directly influencing the flow of credit unless it was on the theory that the greater the number of banks, the better the credit facilities. Speaking of commercial banks, Robert F. Leonard says, "For many years the belief was widely shared that any group of men with a certain, and generally rather limited, amount of capital had an almost undeniable right to establish a bank, and over a long period charters were freely granted." [21] The consequence has often been to raise the supply of loan funds when the supply was already ample, to induce speculative development and finance, to increase the instability of the realty market, and to complicate the difficulty of an ultimate readjustment.

Hoyt, for instance, notes the influence of loose chartering of banks as a factor in realty speculation and collapse in Chicago. The

[20] Savings and loan associations, for instance, were an invention of the 1830's, yet the first law requiring the examination of such institutions was passed in 1875, and such laws did not become general until the 1890's. M. Bodfish, *op. cit.*, Chapter 9.

[21] Robert F. Leonard, "Supervision of the Commercial Banking System" in *Banking Studies,* by members of the staff of the Federal Reserve System (Washington, 1941) p. 198.

easy real estate credit extended by newly chartered banks, such as the State Bank of Illinois in 1835, and the swarm of new banks that appeared following the passage of the State Banking Act of 1851, were in both cases followed by a drying up of credit with the failure of overextended institutions.[22] A similar parallelism of chartering, speculative credit, and collapse can be found generally in the "wild cat" banking era of the 1830's and in subsequent occasions of boom and disaster.

In the savings and loan area, the expansion of the twenties was accompanied by an increase in the number of associations from around 8,600 in 1920 to nearly 13,000 in 1927.[23] In spite of the chartering of federal savings and loan associations since 1933, the number of all operating associations at the end of 1948 was only 6,000.[24] In some of the states the percentage fluctuation was much wider than the national total. The number of savings and loan associations in New Jersey, for instance, increased from 939 in 1920 to 1,565 in 1930 but dropped back to 501 by the end of 1948.[25] While this is an extreme case of liberal chartering and painful readjustment through liquidation or reorganization, it shows how the stability of realty credit facilities has been affected by chartering policy.

It is only recently that the chartering power appears to have been used with credit requirements clearly in view. "The convenience and needs of the community to be served" are now important considerations in chartering national banks and federal savings and loan associations, and state authorities have adopted the same attitude. Current policy has been stated as follows: "Out of the harsh experiences of the banking troubles leading up to the bank holiday of 1933 . . . has come the realization that charters should be granted much less freely. . . . As a result of the cooperation of the various Federal and State agencies, it can be said that it is the general aim of all to grant charters only where there is demonstrable need for the bank and reasonable assurance of its success." [26]

On the whole, this statement reflects a restrictive policy result-

22 H. Hoyt, *op. cit.*, pp. 27, 59-60, and 445.
23 M. Bodfish, *op. cit.*, p. 131.
24 Home Loan Bank Board, *Trends in the Savings and Loan Field*, April 1948, p. 7.
25 *Annual Reports* of the Commissioner of Banking and Insurance of New Jersey. Figure for 1948 is from the Home Loan Bank Board, *Trends in the Savings and Loan Field*, April 1948.
26 R. F. Leonard, *op. cit.*, p. 198.

ing from the conclusion that past chartering had been in excess of need. That the chartering power may be used to stimulate the creating of new facilities where the credit supply is considered inadequate is evident in the chartering of national farm loan associations and federal savings and loan associations.[27]

REGULATION OF THE REAL ESTATE
INVESTMENT PORTFOLIO

Although details of institutional regulation as regards different types of institutions vary between state and federal governments and also among state governments, there is nevertheless an underlying similarity in the concepts and methods used. The pattern of investment is established generally by law rather than through examination and supervision, and it falls into the following elements:

(1) *Determination of the character of the investment: creditor versus owner interest.* The preponderant influence of the law has been to favor institutional investments in real estate loans rather than in equities. Prior to World War I, all types of financial institutions were prohibited from owning property except that necessary for the conduct of their business or that taken through foreclosure. Disposition of the latter was required to be made within a few years after acquisition. For the bulk of institutional operations, therefore, real estate finance has meant mortgage loans.

The first important break in this legal tradition came in New York in 1922, when insurance companies were permitted to make direct investments in housing property. Through 1948, twenty-five states and the District of Columbia had made it possible by special statute for their domestic insurance companies to make investments in residential property; companies domiciled in seven additional states have the same power under more general statutes. Beginning about 1945, the movement to permit equity investment was broadened so as to permit investment in other types of income-producing realty. Because of the absence of specific prohibition, such investment was already possible in five states; five others (including the District of Columbia) did not apply their prohibitions to the investments of companies domiciled in other states. The years 1945-47 saw a majority of the states dropping or modifying their old restrictions, and by the middle of 1948, thirty-four states and the District

[27] See Chapter 6.

of Columbia had in one way or another made investment in a wide range of residential, commercial, and industrial real estate possible for both domestic and out-of-state insurance companies.[28]

Generally, the grant of authority in this new field has been broad, with relatively few limitations on the investor. A few states have confined realty investment to cases where long-term leases to business establishments were involved; in some, residential investment is limited to housing built by the investor; but the most common limitations merely define the maximum amount of a single investment, or the aggregate of investments, or the ratio of realty investments to total assets. As might be expected, there are wide variations among the statutes in these details. Moreover, where realty investment is given some special privilege in connection with urban redevelopment, such as limitation of taxes, the right to benefit from the power of eminent domain, or a subsidy to reduce land cost, there are often restrictions on rentals, net income, or freedom of tenant selection.[29]

Starting in the main from the social purpose viewpoint (the first New York law was closely linked with the housing shortage following World War I), the application of the ownership-investment principle has been broadened to that of a general outlet for funds. In this respect, the trend is contrary to what we commonly find, particularly in the federal sphere. It constitutes the one major relaxation in favor of a freer flow of investment along lines dictated by management rather than by government. The movement, however, is yet too new to have resulted in any large amount of institutional investment or any strong influence on the real estate market.[30] It has been, for the most part, limited to life insurance companies, although Massachusetts, New Jersey, and New York allow mutual savings banks to invest in housing either in redevelopment projects or otherwise. A few other states also permit savings and loan associa-

28 Summary based on a digest of state insurance laws published January 1, 1948, by the Division of Law, Office of the Administrator, Housing and Home Finance Agency, and supplements thereto.

29 See, for instance, New York General Laws, c. 892 (1941), c. 892 (1942), c. 234 (1943); Massachusetts Laws, c. 654 (1945).

30 As of June 30, 1949, the total amount of investment by life insurance companies in the ownership of rental housing was reported by the Institute of Life Insurance to be $275 million, with $185 million additional in projects still under construction. Life insurance investment in commercial and industrial rental property at the same date came to $453 million.

tions to have real estate investments of the same types; several states permit these associations to build houses, either for their shareholders or for sale.[31]

There has, however, been little activity under these last-mentioned authorizations. Thus, notwithstanding the opening of new avenues, the mortgage loan remains the predominant type of realty investment for institutional funds. The reason for this no doubt lies in the supposed margin of safety created by the overage of value in relation to the loan and in the covenant binding the borrower for any deficiency. The recent interest in ownership investment has been influenced by increasing doubts about the protection for the institution inherent in a lender-borrower relationship, by a surplus of funds seeking investment, and by the relatively low prevailing mortgage interest rate.

(2) *Restrictions on the type of property on which real estate investments may be made.* As in ownership investment, the kinds of property in which an institution may invest on a mortgage basis are frequently specified by law or regulation. Savings and loan associations are quite generally limited to loans on one- to four-family houses or very small apartment buildings; farm loans are frequently prohibited and loans on commercial and industrial realty are almost always prohibited or narrowly limited. The authority to lend even on residential property designed for more than four families is usually much restricted, commonly by limiting the maximum size of loans in which the bulk of the assets might be invested. These restrictions, of course, reflect an attempt through legislation to preserve the original purpose for which this class of institutions was created. It may be noted that in recent legislation, and proposals for legislation, the tendency is to increase the classifications in which mortgage loans may be made.

In contrast to the close limitations placed upon savings and loan associations, life insurance companies may usually lend upon the security of real estate without restriction as to type of property. Banks, similarly, have very broad discretion in selection, although in both instances loans on unimproved property are sometimes prohibited or restricted.

---

[31] Summary based on a digest of state insurance laws published January 1, 1948, by the Division of Law, Office of the Administrator, Housing and Home Finance Agency, and supplements thereto.

(3) *Restriction on the location of the property*. State banks and savings and loan associations are commonly restricted as to the geographical area in which mortgage loans may be made.[32] The area may be coextensive with the state in which the institution is chartered or it may be limited by the area within a specified radius (often fifty miles) from the location of the institution. Rarely may these classes of institutions lend on property located in states other than the one in which they are domiciled.

The reason for these limitations is threefold. First, it is assumed that loans may be placed more safely in areas with which management may be personally familiar. Second, it is considered desirable to retain local funds to meet local needs. Third, it is often advantageous to retain local markets for local funds. The objection raised in 1934 by the savings and loan associations to the creation of national mortgage associations, which might operate without restriction as to area, is evidence of the dislike of external competition.

Among state-chartered institutions, the life insurance companies alone have generally been permitted to invest beyond state boundaries, and, under certain conditions, beyond national boundaries. Only a small proportion, if any, of the total mortgage investment made by these institutions is restricted to the state of domicile. Otherwise, the common area-limitation is that requiring the company to conduct an insuring business in the states, territories, or countries in which loans are placed. The fact that insurance is sold without geographical limitation makes such widespread activity inevitable. In fact, to prevent insurance funds from being drained from one locality to serve credit demands in another, Texas, as an example, imposes regulations requiring out-of-state companies to maintain local investments in proportion to the insurance written within the state.

Mutual savings banks in northeastern states have generally been allowed to make mortgage loans on properties in adjacent states. In 1949, New York and Massachusetts authorized their mutual savings banks to make or purchase mortgage loans in any part of the United States, if insured by the Federal Housing Administration.[33]

32 National banks have no area restriction; federally-chartered savings and loan associations and farm lending institutions, however, follow state practice in restricting the area of activity.

33 New York Banking Law, § 235, subd. 20, as amended by the L. of 1943, c. 629, as amended by the L. of 1949, c. 545; Massachusetts General Laws (Ter. ed. 1932)

The other class of national lenders were the predepression mortgage bond houses and mortgage guarantee companies. These institutions placed loans and sold their securities without regard to state
lines. Loosely regulated by law, free from supervision as to their
practices, inadequately protected by reserves, and often irrespon-
sibly conducted, they fell victim both to subsequent legal restraint
and loss of public confidence. At the present time, federal restrictions on the interstate distribution of securities are so rigid that the
real estate bond, as formerly known, rarely qualifies for widely dis-
persed investment.

Where ownership investment is permitted for insurance companies, there is sometimes a location restriction based on the size of
the city or metropolitan area in which the investment is made.
Where other institutions are permitted to indulge in ownership, location is restricted to the state of domicile.

(4) *Limitation of the proportion of assets available for realty
investment.* The mortgage loans of national banks are limited to an
amount equal to their capital and surplus, or 60 percent of time and
savings deposits, whichever is greater. The mortgage loans of state
commercial banks are frequently subject to similar, though often
less restrictive, limitations.

The amount that mutual savings banks and insurance companies may invest in real estate mortgages is generally limited in relation to their total assets, but the allowance (often 60 percent or
more) is more generous than in the case of commercial banks.
Savings and loan associations are the only institutions that are required—in contrast to being permitted—to lend on mortgage security. With the others, alternative investments may be listed at length
and, as a group, are frequently given preference over mortgage
loans; with the savings and loan associations, it is the alternative
investments that are restricted in relation to total investment.

Where ownership investment is permitted to institutions, an
investment-to-asset ratio is again stipulated, which in itself would
prevent any degree of dominance of this type of investment. A 10

c. 168, § 54a, as amended by the Act of June 2, 1949. Both of these laws extend the
authorization to cover secondary mortgages guaranteed by the Veterans' Administration and made in connection with FHA first mortgages, according to the provisions
of § 505a of the Servicemen's Readjustment Act as amended (see Chapter 7).

percent ratio on residential investments and a limitation of 3 to 5 percent on investments in other types of property are common.

(5) *Regulations of the loan pattern.* One of the most common restrictions on institutional lending is the loan-to-value ratio. The limitation is strictest for national banks, where it is held to 50 percent on unamortized loans and 60 percent on loans at least 40 percent amortized within the maximum ten-year term. For state commercial banks the limit is frequently 50 percent or somewhat higher, but in twenty-four states no maximum loan-to-value ratio is prescribed by law. For insurance companies the two-thirds ratio is the norm, although the range is from 40 percent in Texas to a 75 percent ratio (where accompanied by special reserves) allowed for insurance companies domiciled in New Jersey. With savings and loan associations, the usual two-thirds limit is now rising to 75 percent of value to conform to the loan-to-value ratio on home loans permitted to federal savings and loan associations. Eighteen states prescribe no legal ratio for savings and loan associations, although in many cases these are not the same states that give a similar discretion to banks. Frequently, lower ratios are set for loans on unimproved than on improved property, and higher ratios for amortized than for unamortized loans.

Also, the term of the loan is often subject to regulation. National banks are limited to mortgage loans of five years or less where unamortized. In many of the states, however, fully or partially amortized loans may run from ten to twenty years and in thirty states no restriction of any kind is imposed on the term of the loan. Insurance companies are not usually restricted as to length of term, and savings and loan associations, when restricted at all, are ordinarily permitted terms up to twenty or twenty-five years, usually with the requirement that loans be regularly and fully amortized. The amount of a single loan is sometimes regulated.[34]

34 Summary statements in sections (1) to (5) are based upon a study, *Legal Maximum for Loan-Value Ratio and for Term of Real Estate Loans by State Banks Generally and to G.I.'s,* prepared by the legal department of the American Bankers Association, July 5, 1946 and a summary of *State Laws Regulating the Investment of Mortgage Funds,* prepared by the Mortgage Bankers Association, May 25, 1945. The description does not cover mortgage loans made by federally-chartered institutions, or insured by the Federal Housing Administrator, or those guaranteed by the Administrator of Veterans' Affairs, for which see Chapters 6 and 7.

REGULATION OF METHODS OF OPERATION

In connection with the regulatory legislation, supervisory authorities (departments or commissions) are commonly established for the examination and supervision of banks, insurance companies, and savings and loan associations. All types of state banks are supervised by the same state agency; savings and loan associations may be grouped with the banks or treated separately; insurance companies are almost always supervised by a separate agency.

The scope and effectiveness of the examining powers vary from state to state, but the substance is fairly uniform. The Pennsylvania banking law may be taken as an example.[35] This law gives the banking department full power to inquire, during the course of its examinations, into the following:

(1) Property, assets, and reserves held or maintained by the institution,
(2) Loans and collateral deposited,
(3) Methods followed by the institution in the conduct of its affairs,
(4) Investment of its funds,
(5) Interest taken in its affairs by the officers, directors, and employees,
(6) Compliance with the law and its charter,
(7) Any other matter bearing on its condition which the department shall prescribe.

Examinations are made regularly, usually at intervals of one year, but special reports may be demanded whenever in the opinion of the examining authorities they may be called for to protect depositors, shareholders, or policyholders.

Depending upon the wording of the statute and the policy of the administrative officials, supervision may be limited to findings of fact: Is the business being conducted in accordance with the limitations of the law and of the charter of the institution? Are the records in order? Is the institution solvent? Under such a view, action may be taken only when the examination clearly reveals insolvency or a violation of law.

35 Pennsylvania Banking Code, §§ 401, 403, 501-4. For the summaries of this legislation the author is indebted to Ralph H. Richards, President, Home Loan Bank of Pittsburgh. *Nature and Future of Public Supervision.* Address before the Sixth International Congress of Building Societies (Zurich, September 1938).

But this narrow view of the function of supervision is probably not widely held. On the basis of a decision of a federal court, the state may regulate "its corporate creatures" in almost any matter in which it sees fit. Again, the Pennsylvania law may be cited to show the extensiveness of the power of the supervisory authorities.[36] Under the banking code of that state, the banking department may take possession of the business and property of any institutions under its jurisdiction whenever it is found that the institution has:

(1) Violated its articles of incorporation, any order or writ issued upon application of the department, or any law of the Commonwealth regulating its business;

(2) Fallen into unsafe hands or is in unsound condition to transact its business;

(3) Impaired its capital below the minimum required by law or by its articles of incorporation;

(4) Suspended payment of its obligations and has not for a period of one year, after due demand or notice by its shareholders, paid any matured share or withdrawal;

(5) Refused to submit its records and affairs to, or its officers or directors have refused to be examined concerning its affairs by, the Secretary or examiner;

(6) Requested the department to take possession for the benefit of depositors, other creditors, and shareholders.

In many jurisdictions, supervisors, by regulation or practice, go beyond the requirements of law in prescribing limitations on managerial discretion. Thus in Delaware, where no legislative limit is placed on the loan-to-value ratio, the authorities frown on unamortized loans of more than 60 percent of value. The New Jersey law does not restrict the volume of mortgage loans to a proportion of time deposits or capital, but this is done by the regulations of the banking department.[37]

Supervisory agencies frequently consider it within their authority to criticize or make recommendations in respect to lending plans, appraisal practices, or other matters relating to the operation of the institutions. After the financial collapse of the early 1930's,

[36] Hackler v. Farm and Home Savings and Loan Association (1934). 6 Federal Supplement, 610. Pennsylvania Banking Code, § 504. See R. H. Richards, *op. cit.*
[37] *State Laws Regulating the Investment of Mortgage Funds,* Mortgage Bankers Association, May 25, 1945.

supervisors tended to broaden the scope of their functions, exerting
pressure on management in respect to lending policy and the liquidation of foreclosed property, thus making themselves a direct
influence on the real estate market.[38] This influence was greatly
amplified through the control directly exerted by the supervisory
agencies over insolvent or frozen institutions.

EFFECTS OF INSTITUTIONAL REGULATION

The primary purpose of the legal regulation of financial institutions is to maintain a watch over their solvency in the interests of
those whose funds are entrusted to them. Regulation has a profound influence on the flow of funds, but in a positive sense the
influence may be greater on their flow into the institutions than it
is on their subsequent investment. Governmental supervision, combined with additional protective measures to be discussed later,
has contributed much to the confidence of the public in financial
institutions, but the influence of supervisory authorities on the flow
of funds into the realty market has tended largely to be restrictive
rather than stimulative. By increasing the conservatism of lending
policies, it has increased the demand for special means for expanding the volume of mortgage credit.

Because the bulk of institutional funds that are available for
real estate finance are subject to stringent geographical limitations,
real estate finance has retained a strong local flavor.[39] The variety
of state laws that regulate the operations of all institutions, except
those operating under federal charter, is in itself an impediment to
the flow of funds across state lines. Even a federal charter does not
completely eliminate local influence since a mortgage is a state
instrument and the restrictions and limitations prescribed by the
state still apply, whether the loan is made by a local bank on conventional terms, or by the same bank subject to federal mortgage
insurance, or by a national bank, or a federal savings and loan
association. The tendency is to discourage the entry of out-of-state

[38] This influence can go far, whether by direct intent or not, toward inducing
lending institutions to support government credit programs. As one mortgage loan
official stated to the author: "We have put our entire portfolio in FHA's because the
examiners never question them."

[39] National banks and life insurance companies, not subject to an area restriction
on mortgage loans, have done considerable trading in FHA mortgage paper. Both
the Federal National Mortgage Association and The RFC Mortgage Company have
also contributed to the formation of a national market.

funds where redemption periods, deficiency judgment limitations, and similar restrictions create greater-than-average hazards to the mortgagee. Pressure to circumvent these impediments and to bring credit to areas regarded as undersupplied has provided another impetus for federal intervention.

The local character of real estate finance is in striking contrast to the national scope of operations in other fields of investment and has placed realty financing at a relative disadvantage as regards availability and cost of funds. Broadly speaking, the states have been unresponsive to demands for more credit; only in the recent limited authorizations permitting direct investment in realty have they been moved to provide new investment facilities for real estate; and here the aim has probably been more to provide financial institutions with an additional outlet for funds than specifically to meet the presumed requirements of the real estate market.

Consequently, the pressure for credit expansion to meet express demands has tended to shift from state legislatures to the federal Congress. Demands for credit for farmers, urban homeowners, and owners of urban rental property have created national political issues; and the federal government has been induced to supplement, through a number of financial devices, funds flowing into these several uses from the customary sources and to compensate for the restrictions on the flow of funds resulting from state policies.

One outcome of the federal government's entrance into the realty credit market has been (through insurance of deposits and share accounts) to place state-chartered institutions under the influence and regulation of federal agencies as well as their own supervisory authorities. Conflict in policy often ensues. The attitude of state authorities may be at variance with the expansionist policies of the federal agencies. Thus, in 1946 many lenders reported that state supervisors disapproved of 100 percent loans to veterans. Even in the federal sphere, the conservative attitude of the supervisory authorities has not always been in complete harmony with policies promoted by other agencies.[40]

Another angle of governmental concern with credit institutions

[40] See, for instance, the speech of M. T. Harl, Chairman, Federal Deposit Insurance Corporation at Quebec, October 16, 1946 (FDIC release) and the *83rd Annual Report of the Comptroller of the Currency 1945*, p. 2. Both statements decried thin equities and urged caution in lending at the time when the housing agencies of the government were advocating precisely contrary policies.

and credit policies deserves mention: it is the creation of competitive relationships through the benefits provided, or the limitations
imposed, by law. If state commercial banks can deal in mortgage
lending, then national banks will seek amendments permitting
them to do the same. If federally-chartered institutions may make
high percentage loans, then state institutions are likely to insist
on the same privilege. One group of institutions may not only seek
laws to its own advantage but may also attempt through governmental intervention to prevent competition from other types of
institutions. Thus, competition among the several varieties of lenders is, to some degree, replaced by maneuvering for a legal advantage. Once started, this provides a rich soil for the growth of
governmental intervention.

CHAPTER 5

The Question of Credit Policy

THE preceding chapters have discussed impacts upon real estate finance that have resulted from the substantive law of real property, the development and execution of public land policies, the growth of governmental restrictions on land use, the vicissitudes of mortgage lending operations, and the supervision of financial institutions. Nowhere, up to the depression of the 1930's, do we find much that could be called an official policy for the financing of real estate or any effort on the part of state or federal governments to use the power to expand or restrict credit as a means for consciously guiding real estate activity.

Throughout the whole period of national expansion, the role of the federal government in respect to real estate was that of encouraging the settlement of the public domain and promoting a wide dispersion of land ownership. Aside from the distribution of land to settlers and land grants to land companies and canal and railroad companies, it provided few direct aids and offered no interference to the functioning of the real estate market or to the efforts of the states to deal with that market in their own ways. Moreover, beyond the continuous demands for greater privileges for homesteaders, there appears to have been neither pressure for federal intervention nor any broadly held opinion that the provision of special real estate credit facilities was within the federal jurisdiction.

During the same period, the role of the states was mainly concerned with policing fraud, adjudicating disputes in private transactions, chartering and supervising private lending institutions, and intervening more directly only when depressions forced them to extend special relief for debtors. Even the "agrarian revolt" of the last quarter of the nineteenth century brought forth no specific plans for a real estate credit system, but rather concentrated its

76

effort on such matters as railroad rates and general monetary reforms.[1]

CREDIT AS AN INSTRUMENT OF GOVERNMENTAL INTERVENTION

After the failure of the early land bank experiments, the possibilities of the use of credit facilities and credit policy as a means for strengthening and advancing a land policy were only gradually recognized. Effective realization, in fact, did not commence until about the time of World War I, and the full bloom was not reached until after the close of World War II.

Renewed interest in credit measures resulted from the growing dissatisfaction with the conservatism of state law in face of changing credit requirements and the apparent inability of the states to cope with the effects of the over-exploitation of land resources. Impatience for reform brought pressure for action by the federal government. And the federal government, considered at the time to be restricted from direct action except in its own diminishing domain, or in situations involving interstate commerce, found that credit could be an instrument for accomplishing many objectives. It could be used to foster a dispersion of land ownership; to maintain small ownerships, both rural and urban; to favor one type or method of land improvement over another, or certain classes of borrowers as opposed to others; and to bring about reforms in land utilization, farming methods, and urban building and planning.

The remainder of this study will be largely concerned with the method by which these objectives were pursued. What is important to note here is that the more direct concern with real estate credit as an instrument of public policy brought with it a number of new considerations. Obviously, more was involved than mere influence on the supply of funds for mortgage lending, although this, of course, remained of crucial importance. First, the more or less negative and impersonal type of regulation characteristic of state law had to be supplemented or supplanted by a more dynamic sort of intervention that concerned itself less with restraint and protection than with needs, incentives, and positive guidance. Second, where the continuing conservatism of state law imposed obstacles

[1] See, for instance, Ray Allen Billington, *Western Expansion* (New York, 1949) Chapter 36.

to the new objectives, some means of circumvention had to be provided—a requirement that clearly pointed to action by the federal government. Finally, if credit was to become the instrument for the positive guidance of real estate activity and land use, special attention had to be given to the terms of credit—the rate of interest, the loan-to-value ratio, and the period of repayment—as the means by which a credit policy might be effectuated and made of the greatest possible benefit to those for whom it was devised.

BACKGROUND OF REGULATION OF CREDIT TERMS

The regulation of the terms under which credit was issued as a means of effecting moral, social, or economic objectives is, of course, not entirely a new thing. Like most other currently used means of control, it reaches far back into history.

The interest rate, in particular, has been subjected to a long and varied scrutiny by government. Throughout the Middle Ages interest carried the opprobrious label of usury and was banned as immoral. Economic compulsion, however, finally overcame the interdiction. Adam Smith relates the progress toward respectability from the statute of Henry VIII of 1545, which had the effect of legalizing interest not in excess of 10 percent, to the renewed ban under Edward VI, the restoration of legal interest with a 10 percent maximum rate in the time of Elizabeth, and the gradual reduction in the recognized rate to 5 percent under Anne. He concludes: "All these statutory regulations seem to have been made with great propriety. They seem to have followed and not to have gone before the market rate of interest, or the rate at which people of good credit usually borrowed." [2]

Thus the offense of usury came to be not that of charging interest, but of charging excessive interest as defined by a statutory limit set in relation to, but not less than, a recognized rate broadly obtainable in the market. Regulation was no longer based on moral grounds but was aimed solely to protect the weak and uninformed borrower from the exactions of an unscrupulous lender. The reasonableness even of this type of regulation was denied by Jeremy Bentham.[3] The Bentham doctrine gradually made headway in

[2] Adam Smith, *The Wealth of Nations* (Modern Library ed., New York, 1947) Book I, p. 89.
[3] *Defence of Usury*, first printed in 1787.

England when the interest rate came to be recognized as being dependent solely upon considerations of risk and the supply of and need for capital. Demand for legal restraint upon the interest rate lessened, until in 1850 the English statutory rate was repealed on all loans except those on real estate and, in 1854, regulation of the mortgage rate ceased.[4]

In the United States, *laissez faire* has never been applied to interest rates with the full logic of the English example. It is true, of course, that by the time of the first colonization of this continent the legitimacy of interest had been firmly established; and, in any event, the needs of credit were so great that a moral proscription could not have been effective. Nevertheless, because the demand for credit so often exceeded the supply, an unrestrained operation of the money market, such as came to be the situation in England, was not considered feasible here.

The principle accepted by Adam Smith—that of the legalization of an assumed going rate of interest—rather than the Bentham principle of absolute freedom has been characteristic of American law. Nearly every state has some restrictive legislation affecting interest rates.[5] The problem in applying this type of regulation is to assure that the going rate is in fact one that is widely acceptable in the market. The danger always exists that legislators will act on the premise that the interest rate can be what government says it should be and that, consequently, the legal rate may be set at a point actually lower than the market will accept. Furthermore, owing to changes in the market, a once acceptable rate may lose its comparability with the going rate even where an original identity may have existed.[6]

Here we find further evidence of the conflict in governmental objective that is characteristic of our system of real estate finance. The development of mortgage law, with its special concern to protect the borrower in time of stress, undoubtedly has added to the risk of lending and has had a tendency to raise the interest rate to compensate for the additional risk. At the same time the legal

[4] An Act to Repeal the Laws Relating to Usury and to the Enrolment of Annuities, 17th and 18th Victoria, c. 90, August 10, 1854.

[5] Francis W. Ryan, *Usury and Usury Laws* (Boston, 1924).

[6] The history of the fixed 4 percent interest rate on loans made under the Servicemen's Readjustment Act of 1944 (see Chapter 7) provides a vivid example of these tendencies.

freezing of the rate at a level unattractive to investors either lessens the availability of loan funds, or leads to the invention of devices that have the effect of increasing the loan yield, or does both.

Thus we find that, even before the depressed 1930's, many farm states were in the midst of a credit famine. In some of them, available capital was much below what was needed, as investment was diverted to presumably more profitable, or less uncertain, fields. For urban property, the difficulties were no less real than for farm property. In spite of efforts to restrain rates, the actual costs of borrowing on mortgage security, including commissions, bonuses, discounts, renewal fees, and similar devices, put the actual mortgage loan rate far above the nominal legal rate.[7]

The states, therefore, found it almost impossible to combine low interest rates, high protection for borrowers, and ample loan funds. As the years passed, the tolerance born of prosperity also passed; and the onsetting depression aroused demands for an equation of these mutually hostile elements.

Along with the interest rate, borrowers found other difficulties in making satisfactory loan arrangements. Owing mainly to restrictions on institutional lending, which again reflected the state's estimate of the hazardous nature of the transaction, loan-to-value ratios were generally low, with the result that the purchase might be deferred until sufficient equity had been accumulated, or costly second, and even third, mortgage financing might be resorted to. Here the effort to protect those who placed their funds with lending institutions ran directly counter to the policy of promoting small ownerships. Again, state legislatures made little headway in resolving the dilemma; and, again, resort was finally had to the federal government to reconcile incompatibles.

Perhaps even more serious was the problem of repayment. Although the repayment of principal, unlike the payment of interest, has never been considered outright immoral, there have, as we have observed, been occasions when it has been postponed or modified by governmental intervention. These repeated breachings of the

7 See Albert Farwell Bemis, "The Economics of Shelter," *The Evolving House* (Cambridge, Mass., 1934) Vol. 2, pp. 367-76. Bemis points out the wide variations in rates among the states as well as their high general level of mortgage interest rates during the 1920's. Some estimates placed the effective interest rate on second mortgage loans as high as 18 percent, while the rate on most such loans appears to have been in the range of 8 to 15 percent.

mortgage contract may have had some influence in establishing the incongruous practice of making mortgage loans—which are essentially of a long-term character—on a short-term basis, in the hope of getting payment before a new catastrophe and a new moratorium intervened.

In prosperous times, and in rapidly growing parts of the country, the incongruity of making a short-term loan for a purpose that required a long term for repayment was not always apparent. Renewals were usually possible, frequently without curtailment at the end of the customary three- to five-year loan period; and, in some instances, an increase in property values actually served to reduce the apparent proportion of loan to value. Depressions, however, brought disaster when they coincided with due dates; and the spectacular waves of foreclosures attending each major economic decline were eloquent testimony that the short-term mortgage loan was dangerous for lender as well as borrower.

Clearly, some other way was needed to protect the lender from the hazards of the mortgage business. At the same time, a method was needed that would allow the borrower to repay his loan by small payments spread over a longer period of years. The experience of some savings and loan associations, mutual savings banks, and insurance companies with amortized loans indicated their greater safety. It was also obvious that the longer the period over which amortization could be extended, the lower would be the individual payment, and the greater the number of persons who could meet it. Thus, a general acceptance of the principle of repayment by regular amortization would provide an important means for advancing the dispersion of land ownership. The states, however, appeared to be unlikely to take positive steps in this direction.

INTERVENTION BY THE FEDERAL GOVERNMENT

With supervision of financial institutions stiffened as a result of the disasters of the early 1930's, the states were handicapped by the rigidity of their own policies which made credit tightest just at the time some relaxation was required. The federal government was drawn into this situation on the wave of popular unrest that demanded new principles to replace old precedents. Many of these new ideas were greatly at variance with those under which the federal government first entered the field of real estate credit.[8] The responsibility that the federal government assumed was twofold. It not only undertook—as a depression remedy—to assure easier credit generally as well as to make special provision for farm and home financing, but, with steadily increasing clarity and emphasis, it also asserted its obligation to provide "adequate" farms and "decent" homes for those lacking them.

To accomplish these objectives, manipulation rather than mere regulation of credit terms was required; and the interest rate, the loan-to-value ratio, and the method of repayment were all of a piece in providing an instrument for such positive action. The courses open to the federal government in making effective use of this instrument were several:

(1) It could charter mortgage lending institutions, using federal funds when necessary to encourage their establishment and to assure their adherence to federal policy.

(2) It could create institutions wholly financed and controlled by government, and thereby set lending terms in accordance with its estimate of credit needs.

(3) It could, by assuming a major part of the lender's risk, encourage private institutions to lend at a submarket interest rate, with lower down payments and longer repayment periods.

(4) It could subsidize interest rates by making partial payments from public funds.

(5) It could actually reduce interest to a negative quantity, by granting subsidies to certain classes of borrowers.

(6) It could, through various fiscal devices, depress the market rate of interest.

In a relatively few years all of these methods have been used, and the scope of each method, once established, has generally been widened far beyond initial limitations. By and large, the methods followed for cheapening credit have paralleled the methods selected for expanding the availability of credit. Before discussing these matters more fully, however, it is important to note how the interventionary attitude shifts from conventional and orthodox theories of credit operations to almost reverse practices.

The first step, whether in an agricultural or urban environ-

8 This was the instituting of the Federal Land Bank System in 1916. See the next chapter.

ment, is to establish, or encourage the establishment of, new institutions, or to encourage the wider use of existing facilities in areas or circumstances where a greater availability of credit is desired. The primary purpose is to augment and direct the flow of funds. Interest rates, while lower than those produced by a scarcity situation, are still recognizable as customary rates for borrowers of good credit standing. In the selection of borrowers the ordinary criteria prevail. The borrower must be an acceptable credit risk, and, generally speaking, the best risks get the best terms.

The second step proceeds, through direct use of federal capital, or of guarantees to private institutions, to create lower interest rates and more liberal provision for repayment than would be offered even to borrowers of the best credit rating for the types of loans involved. An element of subsidy may enter the picture to the extent that contingent liabilities may result in claims on the government and certain costs of administration are carried by appropriations rather than by the operation itself. Borrowers are still selected on the basis of presumed ability to pay, but the possible range of differentiation in terms has been so reduced that all selected borrowers receive about the same treatment irrespective of differences in their resources and capacity.

The third step, by a more drastic use of the methods employed in the second, and with greater evidence of present or deferred subsidy, offers terms far beyond those obtainable in the private financial market. At this stage borrowers are selected because of their need for help and their inability to meet the terms otherwise available; and the better class of credit risks may be excluded from use of the special facilities.

The fourth step eliminates all financial considerations except the need of the borrower for funds. The use of subsidy is outright—either to reduce the effective interest rate or the proportion of the loan amount that must be repaid, or both. The beneficiary may be an individual borrower for farm or home, or the client of a public authority to which the subsidy is granted.

The steps outlined have not always been taken in the order given, nor does the taking of an additional step mean an abandonment of methods previously adopted. Moreover, the stages are not always as clear-cut as described, since frequently there is a blending of methods. At the present time all methods are being used, the trend being toward greater experimentation with the third and fourth.

All fields of real estate finance, of course, are not directly affected, since the emphasis so far has been on agricultural and housing finance. Yet, during World War II extra-market financing was provided by the government for industrial and commercial property related to the war effort, and, in the postwar period, similar facilities were offered to classes of industrial property connected with the drive for increasing the production of prefabricated houses and of building materials for residential construction.

EMERGENCE OF A NEW ATTITUDE
TOWARD CREDIT

The shifting of the government's attitude toward credit terms has been accompanied by a profound, if not always clearly expressed, change of attitude toward the nature of capital. In the middle period between medieval prohibitions and the present type of intervention, the accepted theory was that financial capital represented a pool of savings available for productive purposes, that interest represented the inducement necessary to create the savings, and that the rate of interest was the measure of the incentive necessary at any given time not only to the creation of the capital fund but to the direction of its flow toward the various investment opportunities.

The place of government under this theory (if, indeed, it was admitted that government had any direct concern with the financial operation) was the creation of an environment favorable to saving (by the maintenance of a sound currency and the protection of investors in financial institutions) and the protection of weak borrowers against avaricious creditors. By and large, it was assumed that a pool of savings would naturally be created by the existence of opportunities for remunerative investment, that savings would flow without compulsion into productive uses, and that, irrespective of state action, the rate of interest would be determined by the supply of and demand for funds at any moment and the degree of risk in the particular investment.

The new attitude stems from quite a different point of view. It assumes first of all that, in a highly industrialized economy, there need no longer be any special incentive to save. As stated before the

Temporary National Economic Committee by Adolph A. Berle, Jr.: [9] "When the scientific development which began in 1900 began to reach its peak, we suddenly found ourselves in a state of affairs which is frequently described as a surplus economy, by which I mean that the productive mechanism of the country could produce more than the effective demand. At that point there was no particular need to bribe or cajole or reward anyone for not consuming, because if he consumed everything he was able to there was still capacity left over, and at that point the economics have distinctly changed."

As a corollary to this assumption, it was taken that the compelling factor in the investment process was no longer the incentive to the saver, but the need for capital funds, and that the rate of interest was not to be determined by what is necessary to cajole a saver but, as Berle puts it, by what was needed to get a particular job done. It was the purpose and nature of the investment, not the requirements of the investor, that henceforth were to set the terms of the loan. If the job required a low rate of interest, then that was what it should get.[10]

This attitude will be clarified by further quotation from Berle's testimony: [11] "The noncommercial business, like a hospital or low cost housing, or the semi-commercial business, like middle-class housing, cannot pay the same kind of rate of interest which a commercial enterprise pays. . . . Our first concern ought to be to work out a banking system which can quote a rate of interest which will take the business. If that rate happens to be a nominal one for something which isn't going to make any profit, then that is the rate to quote. If it happens to be, let us say, a 1- or 1½- or 2-percent rate for middle-class or lower middle-class housing which is not being built by anybody today, then quote that rate. If it happens to be a commercial enterprise, making the standard commercial rate, then quote that rate."

Although this theory has not been explicitly stated in legislation, it is implicit in federal credit measures since the Farm

9 U. S. Congress. House. Hearing before the Temporary National Economic Committee (Washington, 1940) 76th Congress, 1st sess., Part 9, Savings and Investment, p. 3814.
10 *Ibid.*, p. 3822.
11 *Ibid.*, pp. 3820-21.

Loan Act of 1916.[12] It became fully evident in the repeated efforts, following World War II, to manipulate the interest rate and other terms on insured and guaranteed mortgage loans so as—despite a contrary market trend—to make borrowing easy for veterans and to reduce the cost of buying or renting housing constructed during the period of postwar inflation. In the process, a new realm of conflict and inconsistency has been created. A financial system based upon, and apparently to a large extent still motivated by, one concept of the investment process is overlaid by demands arising from a wholly contradictory point of view.

[12] See Donald C. Horton, *Interwar Credit Aids Associated with Farm Ownership and Operation,* Department of Agriculture (Washington, 1945) mimeographed.

The Expansion of Federal Influence

THE passage of the Federal Reserve Act in 1913 marked the end of a period in which it was considered that the requirements of real estate finance (and particularly of farm finance) could be attained by general banking and currency reform. In spite of a number of concessions to the agrarian interest,[1] the Federal Reserve Board was hardly established when there were demands for special credit facilities to assure lower interest rates and a more ample supply of credit for farmers.

The main pressure for creating new financing institutions concentrated on the federal government, although a few states undertook similar experiments. For instance, during and soon after World War I, Minnesota and South Dakota established specialized institutions—wholly capitalized and wholly owned by their governments—for making farm loans.[2] These, however, were quite apart from the main current. They set no precedent, and they rapidly sank into the background with the growth of a new federal system.

FEDERAL LAND BANK SYSTEM

Several years of official study and discussion resulted in the passage of the Farm Loan Act in 1916 [3] and the establishment of the Federal Land Bank System. The original characteristics of the System are well described by Sparks: [4] "These new land banks were a distinct departure from earlier land bank schemes in this country. They are entirely divorced from commercial banking and currency schemes, and are purely investment banks, attracting loaning funds

[1] Such as the elimination of banker representation on the Federal Reserve Board, the provision that all notes of issue be governmental obligations, and the favored status given to farm paper.

[2] Earl S. Sparks, *History and Theory of Agricultural Credit in the United States* (New York, 1932) Chapter 15. In addition to these institutions, many state endowment and pension funds were permitted, or directed, to lend money on the security of real estate mortgages (*ibid.*, Chapter 14).

[3] 39 Stat. 360 (1916); 12 U.S.C. 641.

[4] E. S. Sparks, *op. cit.*, p. 115.

by the sale of bonds based on first mortgages and loaning only on first mortgages."

The new Land Bank System also differed significantly from the contemporary state land banks in that it was designed to be private in so far as sources of funds and managerial policies were concerned. The governmental function, in the initial concept, was limited to aid in organization, temporary financial support, and general supervision. This original concept was later modified because of failure to obtain sufficient capital from private sources to permit early withdrawal of government support and because of the unexpectedly prolonged farm depression following World War I, which brought demands for new functions and policies that appeared to be incompatible with private investment. Nevertheless, the cautious nature of the first interventionary step of the federal government and the prolonged discussion that preceded it are especially striking in view of the successively more drastic measures which were later adopted with progressively decreasing opposition.

The Land Bank System, as first organized, was placed under the jurisdiction of the Treasury and made subject to the immediate supervision of a Farm Loan Board. The Board included the Secretary of the Treasury and four members (later six) appointed by the President, one of whom was designated executive officer of the Board with the title of Farm Loan Commissioner (later Land Bank Commissioner). Salaries and expenses of the Board and of farm loan registrars (one for each land bank) were paid by the federal government. Subsequent reorganization (1933) placed the System in an independent agency, the Farm Credit Administration, and substituted for the Board a single administrative officer with title of Governor. In 1939 the Farm Credit Administration, including the Land Bank System, was transferred to the Department of Agriculture.[5]

From the start, the System has consisted of twelve regional federal land banks. The banks were authorized to obtain funds by issuing stocks and bonds (the bonds were exempt from federal and state income taxes until 1941) and to make first mortgage loans to local cooperative borrower organizations known as national

[5] Donald C. Horton, Harold C. Larsen and Norman J. Wall, *Farm Mortgage Credit Facilities in the United States*, Department of Agriculture, Misc. Pub. 478 (Washington, 1942) Chapter 6.

farm loan associations, or to farmers directly or through authorized agents in areas where no such privately capitalized association had been chartered. Originally, land bank loans were required to be for land purchase or productive purposes. Later, as credit became more stringent during the depression of the 1930's, the range of eligibility was broadened to include loans for refunding debt and even for current expenses.[6]

As evidence of the original emphasis on the private character of the System, six of the nine directors of each of the land banks were to be chosen by the local farm loan associations, the others being appointed by the Farm Loan Board, the governing body of the System. A change in attitude toward a more dominant governmental influence occurred in 1923 when the number of locally selected directors was reduced to three and, of the seven-man Board, four were named by the Farm Loan Board.[7] The abolition of the Board in 1933 with the substitution of a single governor and the subordination of the governor to the Secretary of Agriculture in 1939 carried the concentration of government influence still further.

When the Land Bank System was created, the Secretary of the Treasury was required to subscribe to all capital stock in the regional banks not taken up by the public within thirty days. Since little public subscription was made, the great bulk of the banks' initial capital represented governmental rather than private investment. There was a gradual but continuous increase in the amount of stock subscribed by the member institutions of the System until, by the end of 1931, the federal stock investment had been almost retired and nearly all the federal land bank stock was held by national farm loan associations and direct borrowers. During the depression of the thirties, however, there was a new infusion of federal funds. In 1940, as recovery came, the Treasury holding had been reduced from its peak of $125 million to a little over $67 million; but, by 1943, in order to assist the wartime expansion of

6 *Ibid.*, pp. 79, 83-85. The direct loan provisions were not much used. The land banks were also authorized to charter and supervise joint stock land banks, privately capitalized farm mortgage institutions authorized to issue tax-exempt bonds at a ratio to capital and surplus of 15 to 1. The joint stock land banks operated for seventeen years, until their liquidation was brought about by the Emergency Farm Loan Act of 1933 (*ibid.*, Chapter 8).

7 *Ibid.*, pp. 70-71.

agriculture, the government again increased its investment to $120 million.[8] During the high farm-yield years of World War II, reduction was again resumed, and by the middle of 1947 the last of the federal capital was retired.[9]

In addition to the government support rendered by direct capitalization, the Secretary of the Treasury was also authorized to subscribe to the paid-in surplus and to buy the bonds of the banks, thus leaving no phase of the financial operation without governmental participation. Because, at the outset, questions of constitutionality discouraged the purchase of the land bank issues by the public, the Treasury was authorized to purchase the bonds during the years 1918 and 1919 and subsequently also during 1920 and 1921 up to a total of $200 million. Although the doubt was resolved in favor of the land banks in 1921,[10] the Treasury continued to be a substantial holder of land bank bonds through the early 1920's and did not liquidate its holdings until 1926. Land bank bonds were also made eligible for purchase by the Federal Reserve banks, which have acquired them only on a few occasions and held them only for short periods of time. In addition, short-term loans to the land banks have also been made by the Reconstruction Finance Corporation. Subscriptions by the Treasury to paid-in surplus of land banks (authorized in 1931) represented another substantial form of support, amounting as late as 1943 to more than $142 million.[11]

The retirement in 1947 of the federal capital and paid-in surplus put the Land Bank System—so far as its ownership was concerned—in a position comparable to the Federal Reserve System. In spite of this withdrawal—unique in the annals of federal intervention—the continued power to appoint all land bank officials combined with the general authority of the Secretary of Agriculture over the Farm Credit Administration left the Land Bank System completely under governmental influence.[12]

8 *Statistical Abstract of the United States, 1944-45*, p. 374.
9 *The Fourteenth Annual Report of the Farm Credit Administration, 1946-47*.
10 Smith v. Kansas City Title and Trust Co., 255 U.S. 180 (1921), based on Section 8 of the Constitution. See Edward S. Corwin, *The Constitution and What It Means Today* (Princeton, 1940) pp. 29-30.
11 D. C. Horton, et al., *op. cit.*, pp. 79-80, and 82. In June 1947, the Treasury was reimbursed for the last of its outstanding contribution to paid-in surplus (*Statistical Abstract of the United States, 1948*, p. 449).
12 The Hope Bill of 1947 would again have modified the organization by placing

The significant feature in the Land Bank System was the direct use for the first time of federal funds for capital and paid-in surplus. The early provision for Treasury purchases of the land bank bonds was also significant, since it temporarily gave the System a quasi-central banking support rather similar in effect, if not in form, to the facilities given to commercial banking through the Federal Reserve System,[13] and led the way to other kinds of public support in later emergencies.

BEGINNING OF INTERVENTION IN URBAN REALTY FINANCE—THE HOME LOAN BANK SYSTEM

Widespread public awareness of an urban housing problem was first brought about, following World War I, by high costs, high rents, and tight credit. The state of New York at that time made its first experiments with tax exemption as an inducement to house-building activity. Wisconsin enabled municipalities to lend funds to housing corporations. The North Dakota legislature empowered the state to engage in home building. California made state funds available for home loans to veterans.[14] Suggestions for modifications of the federal income tax on mortgage interest and profits on home-building operations were offered.[15] In the main, however, the approach to the problem was through the credit system.

New York led the way with the creation in 1915 of the Land Bank of the State of New York (later changed to the Savings and Loan Bank of the State of New York).[16] This bank offered a reservoir of credit, created by, and available to, the savings and loan associations of the state. During the period between World War I and the depression, institutions of a somewhat similar character were established in other states, notably California, Florida, Massachusetts, and Ohio.[17]

the System under an Agricultural Credit Agency, separate from the Department of Agriculture and directed by a seven-man Agricultural Credit Board; but this measure (H.R. 1677, 80th Congress) was not passed.

[13] See Donald C. Horton, *Interwar Credit Aids Associated with Farm Ownership and Operation,* Department of Agriculture (Washington, mimeographed, 1945) p. 17.

[14] *Housing Problems in America,* Proceedings of the Eighth National Conference on Housing, 1920, pp. 323-24.

[15] For instance, S. 2094, 66th Congress.

[16] *History of Building and Loan in the United States,* Morton Bodfish, ed. (U. S. Building and Loan League, Chicago, 1931) p. 506.

[17] Report of the Liquidity Committee of the New Jersey Building and Loan League, 1931.

Pressures created by the post-World War I housing problem soon made themselves felt on Congress. In this connection it should be noted that, despite the wartime experience of the federal government with government-owned housing, no serious effort was made to maintain this type of activity. In fact the liquidation of its housing, which was ordered immediately after the war, indicated the desire of the government to divest itself of this responsibility.[18] When the pressure for aid was reasserted, it was in the form of demands for improved credit facilities rather than for direct action in the field of construction.

The first of these proposals called for the discount of home mortgages by the Federal Reserve banks and for the expansion of the Land Bank System to cover urban as well as farm mortgages, but it met with successful opposition.[19] During the 1920's and early 1930's, bills were repeatedly introduced in Congress calling for the establishment of a central mortgage bank, with power of loan and discount,[20] but support for these proposals was not widespread. The less ambitious home loan bank plan took precedence and, in the subsequent wave of depression legislation, the idea of a central mortgage bank quietly succumbed.

The earliest discussions of a federal home mortgage credit system came in 1918 and were followed a year later by the introduction of the first bills on the subject.[21] However, interest in federal action waned as the postwar expansion developed and was not revived until after 1928 when serious weaknesses in the mortgage situation had begun to appear. Following a widely publicized *Conference on Home Building and Home Ownership* called by President Hoover in 1931, a bill to create a Federal Home Loan Bank System was introduced and, speeded by the already apparent realty collapse, was passed in 1932.[22] The System was established in the same year.

[18] See Miles L. Colean, *Housing for Defense* (The Twentieth Century Fund, New York, 1940) Chapter 1.

[19] M. Bodfish, *op. cit.*, pp. 207 ff.

[20] For instance, H.R. 10518, 66th Congress; H.R. 8049, 68th Congress; S. 4310, 68th Congress; S. 3013, 70th Congress.

[21] S. 1469, S. 2492, H.R. 6371, H.R. 7597, all 66th Congress.

[22] Federal Home Loan Bank Act, 47 Stat. 725 (1932); 12 U.S.C. 1421 *et. seq.* The Conference had other less immediate, but in many ways more far-reaching, effects than the passage of the Home Loan Bank Act. The beginning of the present widespread public interest in slum clearance, public housing, limited dividend and co-

The new System followed the pattern of the Federal Reserve
System and the original Federal Land Bank System in that it had
a central governing board appointed by the President and a group
of regional banks. These federal home loan banks were authorized
to make loans to member institutions, which might be any state-
chartered institution (savings and loan association, savings bank,
or insurance company) engaged in placing mortgages on houses
and small buildings.[23]

As in the case of the land banks, Treasury stock subscriptions
were used in launching the System, with the great bulk of initial
capital coming from this source. In spite of the introduction of
numerous bills for the purpose, however, the Treasury, through
1949, had not been authorized to purchase home loan bank bonds,
as it had with respect to land bank bonds. Nor were any federal
contributions made to the paid-in surplus of the home loan banks.
Notwithstanding these differences, the Home Loan Bank System
has continued to be strongly influenced by the federal government
in administration and financing.[24]

IMPACT OF THE DEPRESSION

Neither the Federal Land Bank System nor the Federal Home
Loan Bank System was able to cope effectually with the flood of
foreclosures that swept over the nation in the early thirties. Far-
reaching governmental action was taken, and the next decade and
a half saw developments that completely altered the relationships
between government and the public, government and lending institutions, and lending institutions and the public.

The developments were almost wholly federal in character, al-

---

operative housing companies, "large-scale" housing operations, neighborhood planning, and housing for minority groups, may be traced to the reports of Conference
committees. These reports were published in eleven volumes under the title *President's Conference on Home Building and Home Ownership* (Washington, 1931).

23 Membership has been almost wholly confined to state- or federally-chartered
savings and loan associations.

24 According to the *Statistical Summary, 1949,* issued by the Home Loan Bank
Board in May 1949, government stock in the home loan banks at the end of 1948
amounted, for the first time, to less than half the total (49.7 percent). The actions
of the Home Loan Bank Commissioner in 1945 in disapproving the election of the
President of the Los Angeles Bank and the forced merger of the Los Angeles and
Portland Banks, whatever the merits of the cases, indicate the extent of the power
claimed and exercised by the federal authority. (See U. S. Congress. House. Hearings
Before the Select Committee to Investigate Acts of Executive Agencies Which Exceed
Their Authority, Washington, 1947, 79th Congress, 2nd sess., June 12-14, 1946.)

though there was state legislation designed to relieve mortgage debtors.[25] While these state relief measures were often more drastic than in earlier years, the pattern was not substantially changed. The effect of state action was, at best, only temporarily and partially alleviative; its deeper import was negative and aggravating, for the balance of the law, now so strongly tipped in the debtor's favor, threatened to block recovery.

In this situation, the federal government's initial measures were designed to make foreclosure unnecessary by refinancing delinquent mortgage loans on farm and home property. Under the Emergency Farm Mortgage Act of 1933 [26] (and later amendments to the Federal Farm Loan Act), the rate of interest on land bank loans was successively reduced, reaching a minimum of 3.5 percent between July 1, 1940 and July 1, 1944, with the Treasury paying to the land banks the difference between the rate so established and the contract rate—the first appearance of outright subsidy in a federal credit mechanism.[27] The Emergency Farm Mortgage Act also permitted a five-year moratorium after March 4, 1933 on principal payments on the outstanding land bank loans if the borrower was not in default on any other covenant of the mortgage. The interest subsidies were not ended until 1942.[28]

Under the same act, the Land Bank Commissioner, from a $200 million fund made available by the Reconstruction Finance Corporation, was empowered to make farm mortgage loans not to exceed $7,500 but up to 75 percent of value (as against 50 percent for the land banks) to refinance indebtedness, provide working capital, and redeem foreclosed property. An additional $100 million was made available to the Commissioner for loans to joint stock land banks of which one-fourth was reserved for facilitating a two-year postponement of foreclosure of delinquent loans.[29]

This activity was superseded by the Federal Farm Mortgage Corporation (created by the Federal Farm Mortgage Corporation

25 See Chapter 3.
26 48 Stat. 48 (1933); 12 U.S.C. 1016.
27 From mid-1944 to mid-1945 the maximum interest rate to farmer-borrowers was set at 4 percent and, thereafter, at 1 percent more than the interest rate on land bank loans to national farm loan associations.
28 D. C. Horton, et al., *op. cit.*, p. 86. A deferment of principal payments on new loans was later authorized for the first three years of the loan.
29 *Ibid.*, pp. 109-10.

Act of 1934) [30] to which the funds of the Land Bank Commissioner were transferred to provide the capital stock of the Corporation. In addition to the authority inherited from the Land Bank Commissioner, the Corporation was empowered to assist in financing the land banks through an exchange of bonds. It was authorized to issue $2 billion in bonds, fully guaranteed as to principal and interest. The same interest subsidies were made available to loans of the Land Bank Commissioner and the Federal Farm Mortgage Corporation as were provided for land bank loans.[31]

The actions taken in connection with farm credit were paralleled in the field of urban mortgage finance. In 1933 the Home Owners' Loan Corporation (wholly capitalized by the federal government) was established under the directorship of the Home Loan Bank Board.[32]

This, the second credit institution to be wholly owned and wholly operated by the federal government, was granted a capitalization of $200 million and an ultimate loan authorization of $4.75 billion to be used for taking over and refinancing mortgages on one- to four-family dwellings that were either delinquent or held in frozen lending institutions.[33] The debentures of the Corporation were given a Treasury guarantee first for interest and later (when the bonds could not be sold at par) for principal also.

The RFC Mortgage Company, a wholly owned subsidiary of the Reconstruction Finance Corporation, was organized to assist in refunding defaulted mortgages on urban commercial property and, as a bank of last resort, to make new loans on such property. Later, this institution was used to provide support for various other federal mortgage financing activities such as the mortgage insurance of the Federal Housing Administration and the loan guarantees of the Veterans' Administration, by providing a market for mortgage loans made under the auspices of these agencies.[34]

[30] 48 Stat. 344 (1934); 12 U.S.C. 1020. See D. C. Horton, et al., *op. cit.*, Chapter 7, for description of the organization and activity of the Federal Farm Mortgage Corporation.

[31] *Ibid.*, pp. 110-12.

[32] The Home Owners' Loan Act, 48 Stat. 128 (1933); 12 U.S.C. 1461 *et seq.*

[33] Ultimately $3.49 billion of the authorization was used. The HOLC stopped making new loans in June 1936, although lending for repair and refinancing continued. By December 31, 1948, outstanding loans had been reduced to $369 million, and only twenty foreclosed properties were still in the hands of the Corporation.

[34] The RFC Mortgage Company was liquidated under 1947 amendments to the RFC Act; 61 Stat. 202 (1947).

While these operations were getting under way, the government was already concerning itself with other means of reopening and widening the channels of mortgage credit. Adapting the safety-fund device, which had a long history in New York and Massachusetts, Congress created the Federal Deposit Insurance Corporation, designed to insure depositors in state and national banks that became members of the Corporation against loss up to $5,000.[35] The federal government subscribed to somewhat more than 50 percent of the capital stock of the Corporation, the remainder being taken by the Federal Reserve banks, and the bonds of the Corporation were made purchasable by the RFC and the Treasury. Insurance premiums were set at a level expected to cover operating expenses and claims. Close on the heels of the FDIC came a similarly constituted institution for savings and loan associations—the Federal Savings and Loan Insurance Corporation [36] —with a $100 million capitalization wholly subscribed by the HOLC. In this case, bonds that might be issued by the Corporation were neither guaranteed nor purchasable by the Treasury.[37]

Both of these institutions played important parts in restoring public confidence in commercial banks and savings and loan associations and, indirectly, in overcoming the paralysis of the mortgage market. They reduced, although they could not altogether stop, the withdrawal of funds caused by fear and panic rather than cash needs. Through these means, they minimized further liquidation of mortgage loans and paved the way for a resumption of lending activity.

More direct methods, however, were considered necessary to encourage building and to increase the supply of funds for new lending. One means to this end, the recapitalization of the land banks, has already been mentioned. The act that established the HOLC also provided for the chartering of federal savings and loan

[35] The FDIC was created subject to the provisions of the Banking Act of 1933, 48 Stat. 168 and subsequent amendments, 12 U.S.C. 264.

[36] Created by Title IV of the National Housing Act, 48 Stat. 1246 (1934).

[37] It may be noted that, although in both instances the federal investment was assumed to be temporary, dividends were not paid on the Treasury or HOLC stock until 1947 nor were any plans for the retirement of the government stock seriously considered. In 1947, an act of Congress (61 Stat. 773) provided for the cancellation of the capital stock of the FDIC. A bill providing for gradual retirement of the capital stock of the Federal Savings and Loan Insurance Corporation was adopted by the House but died in the Senate. During 1949 no further action was taken.

associations in order to create new mortgage lending facilities for underserviced areas. Provision was also made for federalizing institutions already organized under state charter. The Treasury was authorized to subscribe up to 50 percent of the shares in any one federal association, with a total actual investment of $50 million. In 1935 the HOLC was authorized to purchase shares in federal associations or state associations that were members of the Federal Home Loan Bank System or of the FSLIC. The total share subscription by the Treasury and the HOLC came to a little over $261 million.[38]

Up to this point the Home Loan Bank Board had been the main focus for measures to stimulate nonfarm home finance. The home loan banks were subject to its supervision; and the chartering and examination of federal associations were in its jurisdiction. The members of the Board served also as directors of the HOLC and of the FSLIC. The National Housing Act of 1934, however, created a separate independent agency, the Federal Housing Administration, to give an impetus to new lending. This was to be accomplished by insuring private lending institutions against losses that might be incurred in connection with unsecured loans for repairs to real property and first mortgage loans on one- to four-family dwellings and larger rental housing properties.[39]

The repair loan plan was at first considered to be wholly for the emergency, with all expenses and claims paid directly by the government. As time went on, however, the original stimulative purpose of the plan was forgotten, and the repair loan insurance became in effect a permanent activity. The principal feature of the FHA scheme, both in concept and practice, was, however, the insurance of mortgage loans.

The idea itself was not new. Mortgage guarantee companies had flourished briefly and collapsed spectacularly in the years just past. But many features of the FHA plan were new. First was the initiation and support of the scheme by the federal government—support that involved the provision of initial insurance funds, payment of operating expenses in whole or in part for a five-year period, full

---

[38] Of the total amount of $261 million in Treasury and HOLC shares in insured institutions at the peak in 1938, only $6,093,000 (or 2.3 percent) remained outstanding as of December 31, 1947, according to the Home Loan Bank Board, *Statistical Summary, 1949*, Table 6.

[39] 48 Stat. 1246 (1934); 12 U.S.C. 1422 *et seq.*

Treasury guarantee of the principal and interest of the debentures issued in payment of claims, and provision of a secondary market for insured mortgages, first by The RFC Mortgage Company and later by the Federal National Mortgage Association.[40] The second innovation was the mutual character of the insurance. Examination fees and premiums were paid into the insurance fund (from which claims and operating expenses were paid) by the mortgagors, who shared in the ultimate proceeds, if any, of the particular accounts into which their loans were placed.[41] The third innovation was the substitution of long-term debentures (representing substantially the amount of the claim) for a cash payment in case of foreclosure.

As originally conceived, the FHA was to be merely an adjunct to the existing mortgage credit system, operated strictly on a pecuniary basis. While the credit under the plan was to be liberal, with loan-to-value ratios up to 80 percent, low interest payments, with amortization spread over twenty years for owner-borrowers (on one- to four-family houses) and longer for rental housing, risk was to be carefully measured and the terms of the loan patterned in accordance. Moreover, the plan was expected to become fully self-supporting as to payment of claims and operating expense out of fees and insurance premiums, an end accomplished after the first few years of operation.[42]

Once adopted and successfully operating, however, the insurance idea opened possibilities of federal intervention far beyond original contemplations. The first step in this process was taken in 1938 when, by insuring up to 90 percent the twenty-five-year mortgage loans on newly constructed houses valued at $6,000 or less, the insurance device was used as a means for directing credit into a specialized sector of the total market. The further uses to which

[40] An institution organized in 1938 under Title III of the National Housing Act, with capital furnished by the Reconstruction Finance Corporation, 48 Stat. 1246 (1934); reconstituted by 62 Stat. 1206 (1948); 12 U.S.C. 1716 *et seq.*, familiarly referred to as "Fanny May," from the initials FNMA.

[41] The first payment on these accounts was made in 1944. See the *Eleventh Annual Report of the Federal Housing Administration*, p. 8.

[42] Although some income from fees and premiums had been used to pay operating expense prior to mid-1939, at that time all appropriations from public funds for that purpose ceased. Because of economic conditions prevailing during the period covered, claims, of course, have been light. The combined capital and operating reserves of all insurance accounts by the end of 1948 amounted to $200,369,176 (*Fifteenth Annual Report of the Federal Housing Administration*, p. 19).

the idea has been put, and the changes in the original business approach involved, will be reviewed in the following chapters.

SECONDARY IMPACTS OF THE DEPRESSION

Without doubt, the measures described above contributed to the moderation and reversal of the deflationary movement and also greatly augmented the sources of real estate credit. The latter was accomplished not only through the new lending agencies but also through the expansion of realty lending by existing institutions, particularly commercial banks and mortgage companies, as a result of FHA operations.[43]

Federal intervention, however, did not cease at this point. Two situations of profound significance had developed. First, through the HOLC, the Federal Farm Mortgage Corporation, and the numerous measures for direct relief, precedents had been established for granting federal aid to the individual in time of emergency—a term, as later discovered, capable of a wide range of definition. Second, the persistence of the depression brought to the fore social and economic inequities which were viewed as insoluble by the relatively unplanned processes of state and private action but capable of yielding to federal action. Since the best avenue of federal intervention lay in the monetary power in the Constitution, as broadly interpreted in the land bank decision, the forthcoming devices for coping with these situations were mainly financial in character. Unlike the facilities provided through the land banks, the home loan banks, and the FHA, which were broadly available to all applicants without distinction except as to their credit standing, the new approach concerned itself with special groups whose resources were so inadequate as to mark them for special aid and benefit. Of note are the operations of the Farm Security Administration, which brought aid to special groups of farmers and rural

43 Mortgage companies, in particular, were assisted by the FHA program in increasing their market for selling mortgages, since FHA processing and regulations resulted in a relatively standardized transaction with security appraised as well as guaranteed by a disinterested governmental agency. These companies, which are generally not supervised by state or federal regulatory agencies, use a comparatively small fund of capital and borrowings for originating mortgage loans to be sold to long-term investors. These institutions found the market for their mortgages expanded from a local to a national scale when the purchasers could rely on the FHA guarantee rather than on their own investigations.

workers, and the United States Housing Authority, which had for its province special groups of urban tenants.

The Farm Security Administration grew out of the Emergency Relief Appropriations Act of 1935 [44] which, among other things, provided for "rural rehabilitation and relief in stricken agricultural areas" and included loans "to finance, in whole or in part, the purchase of farm lands and necessary equipment by farmers, farm tenants, croppers, or farm laborers." After a number of changes in policy and name, the FSA was established in the Department of Agriculture to carry out these functions as defined in the Bankhead-Jones Farm Tenant Act of 1937,[45] and as provided for in subsequent relief appropriation acts. Under the tenant purchase program, loans are made at 3.5 percent interest for forty years—terms much more liberal than are available in the private lending market; and in some cases payments for interest and principal may be mainly on the basis of a percentage of products sold.

Like the FSA, the USHA was an outgrowth of emergency measures taken early in the depression. RFC loans to limited dividend housing companies engaged in providing "low-rental" housing were provided for in the Emergency Relief and Construction Act of 1932.[46] Later this power was transferred to the newly formed Public Works Administration, where, due to a lack of borrowers who could meet the requirements of that agency, the loan facilities were dropped in favor of direct building operations. Under this plan, 45 percent of the investment was written off as an outright grant with the remainder to be recaptured from the rental income of the property over sixty years at 3 percent interest, title remaining in the federal government.[47] In this way "public housing," as it came to be known, was born; and at once pressure developed for a permanent and more generous means for providing new housing for underprivileged urban families.

In 1937, after the passage of the United States Housing Act,[48]

44 49 Stat. 115 (1935). See D. C. Horton, et al., op. cit., Chapter 9.

45 50 Stat. 522 (1937); 60 Stat. 1072 (1946); 7 U.S.C. 1000-1006.

46 47 Stat. 709 (1932); 39 U.S.C. 277; 48 Stat. 351 (1934); 5 U.S.C. 796.

47 The authority of the PWA to engage in housing operations came through the National Recovery Act of 1933, 48 Stat. 200-201 (1933); 40 U.S.C. 8, 402. See Miles L. Colean, *American Housing* (The Twentieth Century Fund, New York, 1944) pp. 276-77.

48 50 Stat. 888 (1937); 42 U.S.C. 1401 *et seq*. See Charles Abrams, *The Future of Housing* (New York, 1946) Chapter 20, for a complete description of the USHA and its methods of operation.

this function was placed in a new agency, the United States Housing Authority, subject to the general supervision of the Secretary of the Interior. Henceforth, construction, ownership, and operation of public housing properties were to be in the jurisdiction of specially constituted local housing authorities. The USHA was empowered to make loans to these authorities representing 90 percent of the cost and to pay annual subsidies which in effect might meet, or more than meet, the carrying charges on the loans. The municipalities were required to contribute annual amounts equivalent to 20 percent of the federal payments. Local contributions might be, and usually were, in the form of property tax abatements rather than of cash outlays.

As the plan developed, it was discovered that loans and annual payments from the federal government often provided a sufficient guarantee to permit local authorities to finance their housing projects by offering their own bonds at rates lower than those at which the federal government could borrow. This condition was made possible by the fact that local authority bonds were exempt from federal income taxes and resulted in a further federal subsidy in lost tax receipts. The initial legislation in 1937 authorized $800 million in loans and a maximum of $28 million a year in annual subsidies to finance these local public housing projects. The bulk of this had been contracted for at the outbreak of World War II.

Through these several means, the federal government discovered that credit could be used not only to better the living conditions of selected groups but also to accomplish social objectives not directly related to a financial transaction. A few examples will suffice for illustration. In connection with the farm loan agencies, it was found that credit might serve as a tool for broad agricultural policy. The subsidized urban housing program was used as a means of applying certain federal labor policies in strictly local situations.[49] The mortgage insurance program provided a means of directing credit in favored price ranges, and of imposing federally-prescribed standards for land planning, construction, and design upon the users of the system.

[49] Except on government construction contracts, payment of prevailing wages, application of wage-hour laws, barring of "kick-backs," prohibition of racial discrimination, etc., all were beyond the reach of the federal government because no interstate commerce factor was present. See C. Abrams, *op. cit.*, p. 273.

Impact of World War II

In 1940 economic conditions had improved sufficiently to dull the demand for further intervention and a trend toward withdrawal of the federal government's influence in realty finance was evident. And also in 1940, the Federal Land Bank System, with the government stock retired from the majority of the banks, gave indications of soon being self-sufficient. The Federal Home Loan Bank System at least held the hope of doing the same. The FHA was operating without further direct appropriations and showed a strong likelihood of continuing to be a self-sustaining institution. The Federal Farm Mortgage Corporation and the HOLC were being liquidated. The FSA was operating in a very restricted field. The USHA had practically reached its initial limits, and Congress had refused its insistent requests for an additional authorization.

The upsurge of war preparations early in 1941, followed by the concentration on war production late that year, violently reversed this trend. It was soon concluded that lending operations based on customary risk considerations would not supply the credits necessary for the industrial expansion and the related housing that were required to meet the demands of war. In many cases, manufacturing plants were built directly with government funds. In other cases, liberal credit was provided by a new RFC subsidiary, the Defense Plants Corporation.[50] While private institutions were not absent from the program, the bulk of the load was carried, one way or another, through federal activity. Government funds were appropriated (following the precedent of World War I) for temporary and permanent housing needed to shelter war workers.[51] Federal funds were also made available for "community facilities"—roads, sewers, water extensions, nursery schools, shopping centers, and the like.[52] In addition, a new part (Title VI) was added to the National Housing Act. This created a nonmutual insurance system (from which the concept of "economic soundness" was omitted) and provided a special fund for the purpose of insuring 90 percent mort-

[50] Created August 22, 1940, under § 5d of the RFC Act, 15 U.S.C., § 606b.
[51] These powers for the most part were conferred by the Lanham Acts, 54 Stat. 1125 (1940); 42 U.S.C. 1521.
[52] The Second Lanham Act, 55 Stat. 361 (1941); 42 U.S.C. 1521, 1523.

gage loans on housing for war workers when the loans were made either to builders or home buyers by private lending institutions. Most of the privately built wartime housing was financed in this way.[53]

A year later, construction not directly related to the war effort was drastically curtailed through exercise of the war powers delegated to the War Production Board.[54] The field of mortgage credit operations was greatly narrowed and numerous imbalances were created. The sharp competition for loans that developed within the restricted market, as well as the forced buying of houses, as units were shifted from the controlled rental market to a free sales market, set loose unforeseen inflationary forces.

In 1942 the housing agencies of the federal government—the Federal Home Loan Bank Board, the FHA, the USHA (with name changed to Federal Public Housing Authority), and various war-born housing activities—were combined by executive order into a National Housing Agency.[55] To this new superagency was given a novel function which, though limited to wartime, had far-reaching future significance. This function was "programming," or determining the location, amount, price range, and proportion of rental to sales accommodations of all new residential construction to be undertaken, and the method—whether by public or private initiative—under which the construction was to be done.

Another significant aspect of this consolidation was the subordination of the peacetime mortgage credit agencies to a general supervision, for the purpose of accomplishing a specific social aim —the housing of war workers. In this environment, the credit system was simply an instrument, and its functioning was geared

[53] Amendments to the National Housing Act, March 28, 1941, 55 Stat. 55. For individual houses for sale the maximum mortgage to which these provisions were applicable was $4,000 raised in 1942 to $5,400. In 1942 the Act was amended to provide insurance for 90 percent mortgage on rental housing properties, with a maximum mortgage of $1,350 per room. 56 Stat. 301 (1942).

[54] Construction of virtually all kinds was required to have WPB approval under the terms of the famous conservation order "L-41," first issued April 9, 1942. Similar action had been taken during World War I. See Bernard M. Baruch, *American Industry in War* (New York, 1941).

[55] *Executive Order 9070*, February 24, 1942. Under this Order the Federal Home Loan Bank Board was abolished and all its functions and those of related agencies were transferred to a single commissioner. The name of the agency was changed to the Federal Home Loan Bank Administration. This action has been reversed and the Board restored. See Chapter 8, footnote 9.

to the advancement of the main purpose, irrespective of other considerations. There were also changes of viewpoint in regard to the operation of the agencies themselves. Thus in the new wartime amendments to the National Housing Act, the requirement for "economic soundness" was purposely dropped; and the making of insured loans was based entirely on immediate needs and current costs with little or no concern with the future.

By the time the war ended the following conditions prevailed:

(1) Practically all new nonresidential construction not related to military requirements or war production was prohibited by the War Production Board.

(2) Only residential construction conforming to the program of the National Housing Agency could be undertaken, though veterans, building for themselves, were given a blanket exemption.

(3) Residential rents were under the control of the Office of Price Administration,[56] except in the District of Columbia which had its separate rent control agency.

(4) The supply of rental housing was continually being reduced by removal of units from the controlled rental market to the uncontrolled sales market.

(5) Building materials, along with other commodities, were subject to price control. Efforts to control the prices of "construction services" had, however, proved unworkable.

(6) The supply of building materials was very short, and no steps had been taken by the government to permit a restoration of production to meet postwar demands.

(7) With the drastic curtailment of new construction, the field of real estate mortgage lending had been largely restricted to the refinancing of existing properties.

(8) Housing demand was already rising rapidly as both the marriage and birth rates increased. Higher incomes and savings from war activities and the special home financing terms given to World War II veterans combined to support an unprecedented total demand for housing.

---

56 In all "defense rental areas," as designated by the OPA Administrator. The towns and cities thus covered comprised the greater part of the nonfarm population. Neither during nor after World War I did Congress enact a rent control measure, except for the District of Columbia. A few states enacted rent control measures during the immediate postwar period. The New York rent control law remained in effect until June 1929. See Edith Berger Drellick and André Emery, *Rent Control in War and Peace* (New York, 1939).

The beginning of the war found large sectors of realty finance subject to government control or influence; at its conclusion both had been vastly expanded. The extension of federal intervention during the thirties made further extension easier during the war. The suggestion of withdrawal evident in 1940 was lost amid the demands of this greatest in a long series of emergencies.

Postwar Emergency Measures

THE end of World War II brought no change in the direction of federal policy, which was toward greater participation in, and control over, the mortgage credit facilities and activities of the country. In addition, in the related fields of construction, operation of rental housing, and sale of new dwellings, certain extraordinary controls of the war period were adapted to temporary postwar situations. Somewhat less drastic measures in the field of credit were adopted as accessories to the emergency programs.

In September 1945, immediately after the collapse of Japan, the Administration, fearing heavy unemployment, released controls on industrial and commercial construction. Residential construction was purposely held back because of the presumed greater job-giving advantages of other types of building. However, the generally rapid reconversion of American industry to peacetime production, the maintenance of personal incomes, and the rise in the nation's marriage rate made it evident within a few months that the housing situation and not unemployment was to be the nation's critical domestic problem. It is not pertinent here to go into details of the planning and counterplanning that ensued. It is enough to note that, by the spring of 1946, all building and real estate activities were more completely under surveillance and control than during the war. And, as a consequence, real estate finance was equally influenced by governmental action.

The pattern of postwar emergency intervention by the federal government consisted of an elaboration of devices developed before and during the war: the creation of credit facilities for special groups of borrowers; the direction of credit into certain lines, through insurance and guarantees; the restriction of mortgage credit outlets through control over new construction; the use of federal and state funds where other means seemed inadequate to achieve the ends of public policy; the maintenance of priorities for the benefit of specific parts of the population; and the maintenance of controls over the rental and management of rental housing. From 1944 to 1947, the attention of the federal government (so far as it was concerned with emergency measures in construction and real estate finance) was focused on four pieces of legislation: (1) the Servicemen's Readjustment Act (the so-called "G.I. Bill of Rights"),[1] (2) the Veterans' Emergency Housing Act (the Patman Act),[2] (3) the Price Control Extension Act of 1946,[3] and (4) the Housing and Rent Act of 1947.[4]

At the same time, the strands of a longer-term housing and credit policy were being more deliberately woven. The present chapter is concerned only with the emergency measures and their impacts, while the succeeding chapter discusses the synthesis of these with longer-term action.

SERVICEMEN'S READJUSTMENT ACT

Of the immediate postwar measures, the first and probably the most significant for the future was the enactment of the Servicemen's Readjustment Act of 1944, Title V of which provided for a system of government guarantees making possible 100 percent financing for farms, homes, and business ventures.

Under this plan, as first adopted in June 1944, the Administrator of Veterans' Affairs was authorized (for a period of ten years after the end of the war) to guarantee as much as 50 percent of a loan, up to a $2,000 maximum amount, made to a veteran of World War II. No equity investment was required. In fact, the avowed purpose of the Act was to make such investment unnecessary. State legislation was quickly passed to permit state-chartered institutions to participate in the operation. Thus, 100 percent loans became possible on properties valued as high as $6,000, where the lender made a conventional loan of two-thirds of value and added the maximum guaranteed amount. On dwellings financed with Federal Housing Administration insured first mortgages, the Act also authorized the guarantee of second mortgages up to 20 percent of the value or a maximum of $2,000. The amortization period in both cases was set at twenty-five years, except for farm property,

1 59 Stat. 626 (1944); 38 U.S.C. 693 et seq.
2 60 Stat. 207 (1946); 50 App. U.S.C. 1821-33.
3 60 Stat. 664 (1946); 50 U.S.C. 901 et seq.
4 61 Stat. 193 (1947); 50 App. U.S.C. 1881 et seq.

where forty years was permissible. Interest on guaranteed loans was set by the statute at 4 percent.

Amid the subsequent inflation of realty prices, it was soon evident that the $2,000 maximum guarantee would be ineffectual if the objectives of the Act were to be realized. In amendments passed in December 1945, the maximum guaranteed amount for home loans was accordingly raised to $4,000, now making 100 percent financing possible for a property valued at $12,000 or less, where a conventional loan for two-thirds of value was combined with the guaranteed amount, and $20,000 where the plan for combination FHA-VA loans was utilized. The same amendments limited the eligible lenders to institutions regularly examined by state or federal agencies.

Some novel features of this Act deserve mention. Although a loan was automatically guaranteed when granted, it was required that the appraisal, and consequently the determination of the maximum amount of the loan, be made by an appraiser approved by the Veterans' Administration. In contrast to the FHA method of reimbursing an insured lender with long-term debentures in case of default and foreclosure, the veterans' loan plan provided for a cash payment on default of an amount not in excess of the guaranteed amount of the original loan, reduced or increased as that amount might be in proportion as the total loan outstanding had been reduced or increased; or, at his option, the Administrator of Veterans' Affairs might take an assignment of the mortgage and pay the obligation in full.

The scheme thus provided full debt financing for the acquisition or refinancing of real property with what was in effect a guarantee by government of the lender's risk. It resulted in a financial procedure in which the function of the lender was reduced almost to that of a disbursing and collecting agency of the government.

The plan had other unique aspects in its relation to the borrower. Plainly, it carried forward the idea of special facilities for special beneficiaries already established in the provisions for farm security and urban public housing. But more than this, it introduced a new kind of protective governmental scrutiny and control of the financial transaction: the veteran was barred from acquiring property under a "G.I." mortgage where the purchase price was in excess of the value of the property as fixed by the approved appraiser, irrespective of his willingness or ability to pay the excess amount.

VETERANS' EMERGENCY HOUSING PROGRAM

Early in February 1946, the President, having already partially restored wartime construction controls and vested his wartime powers to regulate construction in the newly created Office of the Housing Expediter, recommended an elaborate and radical legislative program aimed to increase further the authority of the Expediter in dealing with the housing shortage.

The first phase of this program involved appropriations for federally-financed temporary dwelling units to be operated by educational institutions, localities, or the Federal Public Housing Authority for housing the families of veterans. Nearly 266,000 units were provided during 1946 and 1947 under this program.[5]

Late in May 1946, Congress passed the Veterans' Emergency Housing Act of 1946.[6] This Act, which in many ways was more far reaching in its control over the housing supply than any previous legislation, contained the following principal features:

(1) It confirmed and extended until the end of 1947 the wartime powers of the President to issue priorities, to prohibit proposed construction, and to make allocations of building materials, all of which already had been delegated to the Expediter. Large powers of direction over the actions of other governmental agencies (FHA, the Office of Price Administration, Civilian Production Administration), in so far as they affected the veterans' housing situation, were also granted to the Expediter.[7]

(2) It authorized the fixing of prices on all newly constructed houses (but not, as had been requested, on houses completed before the date of enactment, except as such prices might have been established in priority agreements).

(3) It provided preferences for veterans of World War II in either rental or purchase of newly completed housing accommodations.

5 Senate Report No. 892, 81st Congress, 1st sess., p. 28. As of March 31, 1949, a reported 123,000 units had been transferred to educational institutions and 196,600 units were owned by the federal government.

6 60 Stat. 207 (1946); 50 U.S.C. 1821 *et seq.*

7 The President made the controls granted by the Act more effective by combining the functions of the National Housing Agency with those of the Office of the Housing Expediter through the appointment of a single official to administer both.

(4) It renewed until June 1947 the war housing insurance provisions of the Federal Housing Administration (Title VI of the National Housing Act), limiting their use to builders of housing for veterans (in place of workers in war industries), setting the interest rate at 4 percent on mortgages so insured, and raising the maximum amount of an insurable mortgage to meet current increases in cost.[8]

(5) It authorized the Reconstruction Finance Corporation to grant subsidies to manufacturers, up to a maximum amount of $400 million, in the form of premium payments for increases in the production of building materials.

(6) It authorized (again through the RFC) the making of production loans and the guaranteeing of markets for a maximum of 200,000 prefabricated dwellings and for what the Act called "new type" materials.

The effect of this Act, combined with the retained control of rents and operation of the veterans' loan program, was virtually to create a controlled realty market, in so far as additions to the supply were concerned. Since no structure could be built without a government permit, mortgage funds, except for the refinancing of existing property, could flow only to the extent and in the directions that government, within the limitations of the law, might determine.

After a twenty-five-day lapse in controls, the Price Extension Act of 1946 [9] re-established federal controls over rents and prices. A fear of mass evictions and rapidly rising rents led to the re-enactment of rent controls with only very minor changes from the wartime legislation.

FAILURE OF THE EMERGENCY PROGRAM

On assuming his authority, the Housing Expediter forecast the initiation of 950,000 new permanent dwellings during 1946, most of which were to be available to veterans at prices not over $6,000, or at rentals not exceeding $50 a month. By the fall of the year it was evident not only that this total would not be reached but also that the number of houses completed would fall far short of what

[8] The FHA Commissioner was authorized to permit maximum mortgages of $8,100 on houses for sale and $1,800 per room for rental properties, where necessary to meet increased costs.

[9] 60 Stat. 664 (1946); 50 U.S.C. 901 et seq.

might be estimated on the basis of units actually started.[10] Moreover, it was clear that the prices of finished houses would much exceed the Expediter's calculations. The subsidy program had failed both to ease the price situation or measurably to affect the volume of materials production.[11] The guaranteed market program for prefabricated houses got under way too late to have any influence at all on the year's supply of new houses.[12] Faced with this situation, the Expediter called for more liberal use of government credit and more drastic controls both of prices and construction and resigned when his demands were not met. The machinery of control was then subjected to a process of gradual dismantlement.

Many reasons may be given for this failure, but nearly all are ultimately traceable to the shortage of materials and the increased cost of building.[13] Serious strikes in the coal, steel, and shipping industries, which occurred in the first part of 1946, contributed to the materials shortage and the rising level of costs. More pertinent, however, were certain features of the program itself. The combination of an unrestricted wage policy and a rigid price policy caused serious distortions in profit margins among various optional items of manufacture and retarded the increase in materials production. At the same time, the housing program, through priorities and allocations of materials and insured loans to builders, greatly augmented the number of houses started; and the provision for 100 percent mortgage loans to veterans added greatly to the number of buyers and assured sales for all housing that might be produced. Inevitably, the extraordinary pressure on the materials supply

[10] The figures for the year were approximately 670,500 permanent dwelling units started and 437,000 completed (*Construction,* Bureau of Labor Statistics, February 1948, Table 4, p. 5).

[11] By the end of the year only about $13 million of subsidy payments had been disbursed from a total of around $50 million in commitments. Total payments were in excess of $30 million, according to information obtained from the Office of the Housing Expediter.

[12] During 1946, shipments of prefabricated dwellings amounted to about 37,200 units, of which few if any benefited from guaranteed market contracts. Up to June 1947, when the guaranteed market program had neared its end, it comprised less than 90,000 units for completion during 1947 and 1948 (Office of the Housing Expediter, *Monthly Bulletin,* June 1947).

[13] Wholesale prices of building materials increased 37 percent between VJ Day and the end of 1946; in the same period hourly earnings in building construction increased 14 percent. These figures, however, do not adequately represent the increase in total building costs which, because of the added effects of delays and low productivity, probably rose from 40 to 60 percent above end-of-the-war levels. The upward movement continued during 1947 and 1948.

brought about first a lengthening of the time of completion and then a sharp decline in the number of starts.

It soon became evident that in an effort of this kind one sector of the economy could not be subjected to regulation and direction by the government while the remainder became increasingly free of official restraint. In his attempt to make the housing controls effective, the Expediter was more and more forced to consider sanctions that affected other industries: automobiles, furniture and household appliances, industrial and commercial building, public works, and the export trade. In the end there were only two choices: resort to a much more fully planned and regulated economy, or abandonment of the housing program. With the removal of commodity price controls in November, and with the resignation of the Expediter and revision of regulations in December 1946, it was evident which alternative had been taken.

Retreat from Control

The official veterans' housing program, as revised for 1947, replaced the priorities system by a federal permit system and ceiling prices for new homes by a limitation on floor area. Premium payment agreements for building materials were not extended, and all but two of the existing agreements were withdrawn. The market guarantee program for prefabricated houses and new materials was continued on a diminishing scale. Allocation of raw materials was discontinued after the first quarter of 1947, and, while limitations on nonresidential building construction were maintained, they were on a slightly more generous basis.

In mid-1947 the Housing and Rent Act of 1947 [14] repealed all but a few of the emergency powers conferred upon the Housing Expediter. The only remaining provisions of the Veterans' Emergency Housing Act related to continued veterans' preference for occupancy of new housing units and extension of Title VI of the National Housing Act. Control over nonresidential construction was limited to the relatively unimportant category of buildings for amusement and recreation purposes.

The Housing and Rent Act of 1947 took a step toward decontrol of rents by exempting new construction along with other minor categories of rental accommodations, permitting increases

14 61 Stat. 193 (1947); 50 U.S.C. 1881 *et seq.*

up to 15 percent for existing units upon voluntary agreement by landlord and tenant on a lease of not less than an eighteen-month term from the passage of the Act, and providing for decontrol as of February 29, 1948.

In spite of the general tendency of this legislation to remove war and early postwar restraints on construction, the idea of financial facilities for special groups was persistent. In the summer of 1947 the special class of mortgage insurance for veterans' housing under Title VI of the National Housing Act was extended, and a provision was added for FHA insurance of commercial loans to manufacturers of prefabricated houses.

Although the Housing and Rent Act of 1947 anticipated rent decontrol at the end of February 1948, the control powers of the Housing Expediter were extended for another fifteen months from March 30, 1948.[15] Apartment hotels and single family houses rented for the first time were exempt from control, and other minor modifications of the control regulations were made.

In early 1948 another step in the gradual retreat from emergency programs was taken when the FHA Title VI insurance program for one- to four-family homes was permitted to lapse. The Title VI rental housing program, however, was extended with only slight modifications.

COMPLETE REMOVAL OF FEDERAL CONTROLS PROVES DIFFICULT

Termination of the last surviving emergency control programs was again deferred in early 1949 when the Housing and Rent Act of 1949 [16] extended both the veterans' preferences for occupancy of new accommodations and the federal program of rent controls until mid-1950.

At the time of passage of this legislation, however, the conviction was growing that by mid-1950 the federal government should be able to divest itself of responsibility for rent controls, placing control of individual areas under local authority and action. In anticipation of that time, three methods were provided by the 1949 legislation for elimination of federal controls in individual localities:

[15] 62 Stat. 93 (1948); 50 U.S.C. 1881 *et seq.*
[16] Public Law 31, 81st Congress.

(1) Decontrol by the Housing Expediter, either on his own initiative or in response to a recommendation of the local advisory board. In these instances, future recontrol was permissible at the Expediter's discretion.

(2) Decontrol by resolution of the local governing body, with approval of the governor of the state, declaring rent control no longer necessary. No recontrol power was provided in these cases.

(3) Decontrol of the entire state or specific localities by passage of a state law declaring rent control no longer necessary. Possibilities of recontrol in these cases depended on the provisions of the decontrol law.

In addition, federal control could be replaced by state or local control established by state law and properly certified by the governor of the state.

By early October 1949, a total of 189 entire defense rental areas had been freed from control, out of nearly 600 such areas in March 1949. Parts of an additional 144 defense rental areas had been decontrolled; and control of rents in fourteen areas in Wisconsin had been transferred by state law to control by the state of Wisconsin.[17]

In addition to the Wisconsin law, which provided for the removal of rent control on June 1, 1950, four other states had made steps in the same direction. Nebraska and Texas had acted to terminate controls in the fall of 1949, with authority for local controls in Texas at the option of the localities. Legislative action in Alabama and Nevada, the former providing decontrol in May 1950, was incomplete. The Alabama legislation was involved in a court test of the legality of the governor's approval; the Nevada law awaited the governor's action.

In October 1949 the federal government was still arranging for disposition of federally-owned housing produced during the war and postwar emergencies. The initial disposition date for this housing had been extended from July 1949 to January 1, 1951. The unsolved disposition problems involved 136,300 war housing units in permanent structures, 188,250 war housing units in temporary structures (including trailers), and about 125,250 veterans' emergency units in temporary structures.[18] Proposals for disposi-

[17] Summarized from notices by the Housing Expediter in the *Federal Register* and other sources.
[18] Public Housing Administration statistics for June 30, 1949.

tion included sale of the permanent units for public low-rent use or private investment and transfer of the responsibility for disposing of temporary units to local governments or educational institutions. However, with the exception of an authorization for the Public Housing Authority to give veterans' emergency units on municipally-owned land to the cities in which they were located, all decisions on the disposition of war housing were deferred in the first session of the Eighty-first Congress, by setting the date for disposition ahead from January 1, 1950 to January 1, 1951.

With the gradual dismemberment of the federal rent control system and the plans for an end to federal ownership of the war and veterans' housing, the series of emergency postwar measures in the field of housing and housing finance drew to a close. The incorporation of some features of the emergency programs into longer-term federal policies and practices, especially in the field of finance, is discussed in the succeeding chapter.

EMERGENCY HOUSING PROGRAMS OF STATES

The same pressures for emergency action that were brought on the first postwar Congress were felt by the state legislatures, forty-seven of which were in session during the first half of 1947. The governments of the various states developed legislation adapted to the specific emergency housing problems of their own populations. For the most part, state emergency activities related to providing assistance to veterans, to relieving special local problems of nonveterans, and to supplementing federal rent control.

The federal emergency program for providing temporary units for the use of veterans' families extended into every state and the District of Columbia. In addition, twenty-eight states adopted veterans' programs supplementing federal activities.[19] There was great variety in these state programs, ranging from the establishment of a state coordinating committee in Maryland to assist cities in participating in the federal veterans' emergency housing program to a comprehensive program in California involving construction of

19 Discussion of emergency housing action by states is based on material prepared by the Office of the Administrator of the Housing and Home Finance Agency for the *Hearings on General Housing Legislation Before a Subcommittee on Banking and Currency* (U. S. Congress. Senate. 81st Congress, 1st sess., February 3-21, 1949). See also "State and Local Housing Programs After World War II," *Monthly Labor Review*, Vol. 69, No. 5 (November 1949) pp. 499-502.

units for rent to veterans, with state and local subsidies, loans from the state to veterans for purchase of both homes and farms, and purchase of federal surplus housing units for resale to veterans.

Other devices enacted that year for assistance to veterans included (1) construction by municipalities of permanent units for rent to veterans in Colorado, Illinois, Kentucky, Massachusetts, and Virginia and construction of units for sale in Milwaukee; (2) provision of land for use of veterans—for building temporary units in Lincoln, Nebraska and in Connecticut, or for building homes to be owned by veterans in Massachusetts; (3) an extra homestead tax exemption in Louisiana; (4) special lumber production for veterans from public lands in Connecticut and New Hampshire; (5) dormitories at colleges in several states; and (6) preferences for occupancy in publicly-owned, state-assisted housing in New York and Rhode Island.

Nearly all of these activities have a specified time limit, such as a five-year period for the homestead tax exemption in Louisiana, and a common proviso that temporary units provided for veterans' occupancy shall be vacated and demolished by a specified date or at such earlier time as the housing emergency is declared at an end. On the other hand some of the benefits for veterans are of indefinite duration, as, for example, the funds provided in California and Mississippi for purchase of farms or homes to be resold to veterans at cost and the specific authorization for groups of veterans in North Carolina to establish housing cooperatives.

In addition to the emergency programs for aid to veterans, a few states adopted plans for emergency aid to nonveteran groups with special problems. California provided state funds for financing housing for agricultural laborers. Rhode Island authorized Providence and other cities to acquire or build permanent housing for veterans and nonveterans. Arkansas authorized cities to acquire federal surplus property to be operated as emergency housing for a two-year period, without restriction of use to families of veterans.

A number of states adopted emergency legislation between 1945 and 1949 supplementing federal rent controls.[20] Most com-

20 Discussion based generally on Carrie E. Hunter, *State Rent Control Laws,* Public Affairs Bulletin No. 62 (February 1948), Legislative Reference Service of the Library of Congress, supplemented by additional information on legislation adopted by August 1949.

mon were laws to enable the state or local governments to act effectively if local emergency conditions developed when federal residential rent controls ended. Some states, however, established state controls of rents for rooming houses, tourist homes, hotel accommodations, or trailers when federal controls over these facilities were removed by legislative or administrative action in 1947 and 1948. And New York in 1945 established controls over rents of commercial and business space when Congress refused to inaugurate federal controls.

Louisiana, Michigan, New Jersey, and Rhode Island enacted residential rent control legislation in July 1946, when federal controls lapsed between June 30 and July 25. New York had previously adopted stand-by controls to take effect when federal controls expired.[21] During 1947, additional state control programs were enacted in Connecticut, Illinois, Maryland, Minnesota, Missouri, Virginia, and Wisconsin. Texas adopted a rent decontrol law in 1949 which also authorized local rent controls at the option of the local governments involved.

The state of New York established the first rent control programs for nonresidential properties in early 1945. Rents of industrial, storage, and wholesale business properties were controlled under a Commercial Space Act adopted on January 24, 1945, while a companion law, approved on March 28, 1945, brought the rents of retail store and office space under control.

All state programs for rent control included restraints on evictions as essential parts of the control procedure. From these state laws for controlling residential rents emerged two significant variations from the federal program. First was a proviso in some of the stand-by legislation as early as 1947 that localities would be able to declare an end to the state control on their own initiative. Second was the frequent assignment of responsibility for enforcement or adjustment of rent ceilings to the courts, rather than to elaborate administrative organizations.

The New York programs for control of nonresidential rents involved two additional distinctive features which deserve study

21 The first state rent legislation was enacted after World War I in Massachusetts, New Jersey, New York, and Wisconsin. In World War II, Virginia was the first state to enact rent control legislation in 1942, but this legislation expired March 15, 1944, without having been placed in effect.

should the question of rent control arise in the future. One feature provided for rent increases above the legislative maximum if the increase were arrived at by arbitration, written agreement of the parties involved, or a Supreme Court decision. The second feature was that the law made excessive rent charges unenforceable, rather than prohibiting the excessive rentals. While somewhat greater court activity may have resulted from these features, a substantial reduction of administrative expense and possibly greater equity of administration may have been gained.

CHAPTER 8

The Emergence of Postwar Policies

IN 1943, while the war was at its height, both houses of Congress established special committees to consider economic problems expected to arise when hostilities should be ended. The Special Committee on Post-War Economic Policy and Planning of the Senate took particular interest in housing, establishing a subcommittee on Housing and Urban Redevelopment. This subcommittee was well into its studies by the time the first of the emergency measures—the Servicemen's Readjustment Act, discussed in the preceding chapter—had been passed, and its findings became the focal point for the development of the subsequent legislation affecting the building and financing of residential property.

The main lines of this development are found in the testimony of the National Housing Administrator before this subcommittee in June 1944 and January 1945.[1] Proposals called for the provision of market information and technological research in construction, further liberalization of the mortgage insurance device, federal aid for the assembly of land in urban slum areas, a resumption of federal loans and subsidies for public housing, and the perpetuation of the centralized control of administrative policy which had resulted from the establishment of the National Housing Agency. Implicit in the Administration's policy was the view that the housing needs of the country could not be properly satisfied by the undirected operation of the building and financing markets, and that only through conscious planning and direction could excesses be prevented, the public be protected from exploitation, and the best use of resources be assured.[2]

GENERAL HOUSING BILL

Embodying Administration suggestions, a bill proposing a comprehensive federal housing policy was introduced in the Senate in the

1 Testimony of John B. Blandford, Jr., U. S. Congress. Senate. *Hearings Before the Subcommittee on Housing and Urban Redevelopment of the Special Committee on Post-War Economic Policy and Planning* (Washington, 1944) 78th Congress, 2nd sess., Part 4, pp. 1015-63, and Part 6, pp. 1191-1321.

2 *Ibid.*, Part 6, pp. 1296-1320.

fall of 1945.[3] Despite the bipartisan sponsorship of Senators Wagner, Ellender, and Taft, their General Housing Bill raised more bitter controversy than similar measures during the preceding decade and a half. Although not enacted, the bill passed the Senate early in 1946 with no registered dissent and might well have passed the House had it not been delayed by its opponents and finally buried in committee.

The outstanding—and the most controversial—features of the bill were the following:

(1) A provision for the continuation of the National Housing Agency, thus giving to a single Administrator power to determine the operating policies of the Federal Home Loan Bank Administration, the Federal Housing Administration, and the Federal Public Housing Authority. The Administrator was also given extensive authority to engage in economic and technical research, to prepare housing "programs," and to recommend legislation.

(2) Through extensive amendments to the National Housing Act, special formulas for insuring mortgage loans for both owner-occupied and rental properties were provided, under which credit was to be advanced not on the basis of ability to repay a debt but rather on need for a house and inability to pay for it on terms otherwise available. For some cases equity payments were reduced to 5 percent of value, the amortization period was extended to thirty-two years, and interest was set at $3\frac{1}{2}$ and 4 percent, depending on the type of property. A welfare basis for credit was thus clearly enunciated.

(3) A new title to the National Housing Act would have permitted the Federal Housing Administration to guarantee a minimum yield ("yield insurance") on a wholly debt-free investment in rental housing property. A somewhat similar device had been initiated by Canadian law in the previous year,[4] but the principle of guaranteeing venture capital investments was new in government-investor relationships in the United States.

(4) A system was to be created for providing federal financial assistance to municipalities for the purpose of acquiring land in slum

3 S. 1592, 79th Congress. This bill was brought in soon after the opening of a special fall session. An earlier version had been introduced by Senators Wagner and Ellender on the last day of the regular session.

4 Dominion of Canada, National Housing Act of 1944, 8 George VI, c. 46.

and blighted districts, independently of the public housing function, thus greatly expanding the scope of federal grants to municipal agencies.

(5) An expansion of the public housing program, which had been established by the United States Housing Act of 1937, was authorized. Provision was made for financing 500,000 dwelling units over a five-year period.

(6) An elaborate system of subsidized rural housing was provided. In this the procedures of the United States Housing Administration were generally followed, but the proposed system offered subsidies, heretofore limited to publicly-owned rental property, to transactions where ultimate ownership by the beneficiary was intended.

FARMERS' HOME ADMINISTRATION

In contrast to the protracted and acrimonious debate over the Wagner-Ellender-Taft Bill, the Cooley Act,[5] which was equally novel in some of its provisions, passed both houses almost without objection. This Act established a Farmers' Home Administration (confusingly referred to as FHA in official literature) to take over the functions of the Farm Security Administration, along with certain special-purpose functions of the Farm Credit Administration, and to provide a system for insuring loans of the type permitted by the Bankhead-Jones Farm Tenant Act,[6] when made by private institutions.

This insurance plan goes much further in shifting both responsibility and risk to the government than did the Federal Housing Administration or, in some respects, either the veterans' guaranteed loan plan or even the proposed innovations of the Wagner-Ellender-Taft Bill. The scheme is as follows: the government agency handles the initial loan negotiation and transaction for the private lending institution; it collects payments due on interest and principal and transmits them to the institution; it continues such payments from its own funds in case of default; and, when the default is clearly irremediable, it pays in cash the outstanding amount of the loan.

5 60 Stat. 1072 (1946); 7 U.S.C. 1001 et seq.
6 See Chapter 6.

At time of enactment, the plan carried a 2½ percent net interest rate to the lender, a rate justified by the proponents of the Act on the grounds that the security was in effect a government obligation guaranteed at par. It was at least true that government could hardly go further than it had in this Act to relieve the lender of responsibility, servicing cost, and risk, nor could it do much more to assure that the borrower would be guided along lines conforming to governmental policy.

Amendment of the Bankhead-Jones Act in June 1948 increased the interest charge to the borrower from 3½ to 4 percent, raising the net interest payment to the lender to 3 percent.[7] Since October 1947, when the first insured loan was closed, the loan insurance program has gradually expanded; but by the fall of 1949 it had not yet reached significant volume.

Housing Commission Bill and Reorganizaton of Federal Agencies

Under the name of the National Housing Commission Bill, legislation similar to the General Housing Bill of 1946 was introduced in 1947.[8] With the new version, the authority of the Administrator would be somewhat limited by comparison with the original bill, and a National Housing Commission would take over coordinating functions of the National Housing Agency. The substantive provisions of the original bill, however, were altered in minor details only. Congress failed to act on the measure in 1947, thereby letting it be carried over to 1948.

A modified plan for reorganizing the housing agencies, submitted by the President under the terms of the Reorganization Act of 1945, was accepted by Congress in the summer of 1947 when it became apparent that action would be delayed on the National Housing Commission Bill. The plan, which established a Housing and Home Finance Agency under a single administrator, made permanent the centralized direction of the housing and related credit activities of the government, as first accomplished by the warborn National Housing Agency.[9]

7 62 Stat. 534 (1948); 7 U.S.C. 1003 and 1005b.

8 S. 866, 80th Congress.

9 This reorganization plan (No. 3, 1947) also re-established the Federal Home Loan Bank Board consisting of three members. In effect, it accomplished the purpose

1948 LEGISLATIVE EFFORT

The spring of 1948—the second year of the Eightieth Congress—brought renewed efforts to pass a comprehensive general housing measure. The Senate, as in the two previous years, took the initiative, and, once more against feeble opposition, passed a re-embodiment of the National Housing Commission Bill, omitting the section dealing with the administrative coordination of the several housing agencies, an objective already accomplished by the reorganization plan.[10]

A blend of emergency (further extension of the warborn "Title VI" insurance,[11] including insurance of loans to manufacturers of prefabricated houses and of loans for the purchase of houses built by the government during the war) and of the now familiar long-range measures (more generous FHA operations, "yield insurance", subsidy programs for urban redevelopment, urban public housing, houses on marginal farms, and a recreated Federal National Mortgage Association as an outright arm of government policy[12]), this bill was designed to draw support from all quarters. Nevertheless, the measure faced a still-reluctant House of Representatives which, after protracted hearings, hurriedly passed a substitute measure from which all subsidy features were omitted. Congress then adjourned with no agreement on the differing proposals for general legislation. However, compromise legislation entitled "The Housing Act of 1948" was at length agreed upon at a special session called by the President after the 1948 presidential nominating conventions.

This Act,[13] which omitted the controversial subsidy programs for public housing and slum clearance, contained the following principal provisions:

---

of the first part of the proposed General Housing and National Housing Commission Bills (see above) and of an earlier reorganization plan which had been rejected during 1946.

10 S. 866, 80th Congress.

11 See Chapter 7.

12 Up to this time, the National Housing Act still offered the possibility of establishing privately capitalized national mortgage associations (see Chapter 6). The 1948 proposals eliminated this possibility, and reconstituted the then existing Federal National Mortgage Association as a government corporation operated under the jurisdiction of the Reconstruction Finance Corporation.

13 62 Stat. 1206 (1948) and 62 Stat. 1268 (1948); 12 U.S.C. 1701-1747.

(1) The Housing and Home Finance Agency was authorized to engage in research aimed at improving building codes and correlat-
ing the dimensions of building materials and equipment.[14]

(2) Title III of the National Housing Act was completely rewritten
to preclude the possibility of any privately financed national
mortgage association. The Federal National Mortgage Association, established as a subsidiary of the Reconstruction Finance
Corporation in 1938, was thus made the sole possible national
mortgage association. It was authorized to purchase not only
mortgages on one- to four-family houses insured by FHA but also
FHA-insured mortgages on rental property and mortgages guaranteed by the Veterans' Administration after April 30, 1948.[15]

(3) The emergency program for FHA insurance of rental-housing
mortgages was extended until early 1949 with a liberalization of
the eligible mortgage amount to $8,100 per unit. Among the
minor amendments was a restriction which prohibited discrimination against families with children.

(4) The authority to insure production loans for manufacturers of
prefabricated houses, granted to FHA in the Housing and Rent
Act of 1947, was expanded to include insurance of credit to
dealers in such houses for periods intended to cover erection and
sale after delivery from the manufacturer.

(5) A new form of FHA mortgage insurance was created to provide
for the insurance of construction loans for projects of twenty-five
or more single family units. Insurance was limited to $6,000 per
unit and 80 percent of estimated value, and was particularly
intended to assist site-fabrication techniques of construction.

(6) The Federal Housing Administration's original type of insurance of small home mortgages was liberalized by increasing the
mortgage limits for low-value homes, by allowing all mortgages
on new houses to have twenty-five-year terms, and by establishing

[14] Interest in the latter was the result of studies in "modular coordination" initiated some years previously by the American Standards Association under the joint
sponsorship of the Producers' Council (an association of manufacturers of building
materials and equipment) and the American Institute of Architects and based on
exploratory work by the Bemis Foundation.

[15] The Federal National Mortgage Association's legislative history is quite con-
fusing. The original National Housing Act permitted national mortgage associations
to purchase, but not to initiate, insured mortgage loans. In 1938 the FNMA was
authorized to make initial loans on rental properties. In the Act of July 1, 1948, the
power to initiate loans was eliminated, and the purchasing authority was limited to
mortgages on one- to four-family houses insured by FHA, and purchases were restricted to 25 percent of the original mortgagee's holdings of eligible mortgages. The
Act of August 10, 1948 again modified the authority, as stated above, restricting
purchase to 50 percent of the mortgagee's holdings of eligible mortgages.

a special class of insurance permitting a 95 percent loan-to-value ratio and a thirty-year term for mortgages of $6,000 or less on new owner-occupied houses.

(7) The prewar provisions for insuring mortgages on rental properties were modified by increasing the insurable mortgage limits to $8,100 per unit, but the limitation of mortgages to 80 percent of value continued in effect, except that 90 percent loans were insurable where the housing was for families of "lower" income and 95 percent loans where the owner was a cooperative association comprised of World War II veterans.

(8) Reviving a device that had been part of the "Veterans' Emergency Housing Program," the RFC was authorized, on a limited scale, to make loans to housing prefabricators for working capital and equipment.

(9) A new Title VII of the National Housing Act authorized FHA to embark upon a new "yield insurance" activity. Individuals or corporations making wholly debt-free investments in rental housing were to be guaranteed a minimum 2 percent annual amortization of investment and $2\frac{3}{4}$ percent annual yield on outstanding investment. Provision was made for accelerated amortization if the annual yield from the investment exceeded $3\frac{1}{2}$ percent. Indemnification of investors would include cash reimbursement for any deficiency in the guaranteed yield or annual amortization as determined on the basis of annual operating statements, with the limitation that, if aggregate cash indemnifications exceeded 15 percent of original investment, FHA could acquire title to the project in exchange for debentures equaling 90 percent of the outstanding investment. Transfer of the project to FHA on similar terms was also provided for at the option of the investor if cumulative operating losses (not covered by FHA insurance) exceeded 5 percent of original investment. The yield insurance contract would terminate automatically when the outstanding investment was reduced to 10 percent of the original amount and might also be terminated earlier at the request of the investor upon payment of stipulated penalty premiums.

THE FAIR DEAL

It was clear that the Housing Act of 1948 constituted little more than a delaying action on the part of those opposed to the more drastic interventionary measures. Actually, substantial gains had been achieved by the proponents of the comprehensive plan. Centralized direction of the housing agencies (designed to bring FHA and Federal Home Loan Bank operations within the scope of planning) was firmly established. The concept of "economic soundness," originally characteristic of the FHA mortgage insurance operation, had been considerably weakened. The yield insurance scheme had been enacted. A new and more pliant sort of FNMA was created. Direct government loans were made available at least to prefabricators, and a small part of the broad research program was put in operation.

With so much gained, there was renewed pressure for the enactment of the remainder. In his 1948 election campaign, President Truman placed much emphasis on the necessity for federal intervention in economic affairs, and in the program demanded by him proposals for more direct government aid for low rental housing and the elimination of slums were prominent.

Soon after the opening of the Eighty-first Congress in 1949, the legislative battle was renewed. Strategy was modified to provide for separate consideration of the proposals dealing with outright grants and subsidies[16] and of the proposals that offered "aids to private enterprise."[17] By midyear the first set of propositions, under the name of "The Housing Act of 1949," won over spirited opposition—almost successful in the House—and became law.[18] This complex measure contained the following provisions:

(1) For the first time, Congress expressed as national policy the propositions that the general welfare and security of the nation required a remedy for the housing shortage, elimination of inadequate housing, and realization of a "decent home and suitable living environment for every American family." While declaring that private enterprise should serve as large a part of the total need as possible, this declaration set forth the governmental responsibility for positive action for the redevelopment of cities, slum clearance, and low-rent housing in nonfarm areas and for improvement of housing on farms.

(2) A new program of federal assistance to localities for redevelopment and slum clearance projects was initiated. Its execution was assigned to the Administrator of the Housing and Home Finance Agency. A fund of $1 billion was made available for

16 S. 138 and H.R. 933, 81st Congress, later superseded by S. 1070 and H.R. 4009.
17 S. 712 and H.R. 1938, 81st Congress, later superseded by S. 2246 and H.R. 6070.
18 Public Law 171, 81st Congress.

loans through which localities might finance slum-clearance and redevelopment projects which the Administrator had approved. Loans might be made for a period of forty years at the going federal rate of interest, defined as not less than 2½ percent. Temporary loans were also authorized for financing preparation of redevelopment plans. The Housing and Home Finance Agency was authorized to contribute capital grants up to two-thirds of the net cost of redevelopment projects in a community, with the amount of the federal grant to be determined upon disposal of the redevelopment area to either public or private redevelopment agencies.

Although the law specifically states the desirability of maximum participation by private enterprise in redevelopment programs, another requirement for adequately rehousing displaced families appears to restrict the program largely to public housing projects.

(3) The public low-rent housing program was revived and expanded by authorizing additional annual federal contributions to local housing authorities up to an aggregate of $308 million per year for a forty-year period. A maximum of 810,000 publicly-owned units might be assisted under the program, and the contracts for federal contributions were authorized to be made over a six-year period. Interest rates on Public Housing Administration loans to local authorities were established at the going federal rate, and financing by tax-exempt local authority bonds was encouraged by permitting the federal contract for annual contributions to be pledged as security. Construction cost limitations in the original 1937 law were increased to $1,750 per room, with permission for $2,500 per room if necessary. The previous requirement for elimination of substandard units was significantly modified to avoid any federal responsibility for enforcement of the requirement.

(4) The Housing and Home Finance Agency was authorized to undertake a broad program of technical and economic research in the fields of residential construction and finance. This program could deal with construction techniques, materials, or methods and with housing economics and other housing market data. Building codes, standardized dimensions, and methods of production and distribution of building materials and housing components were all specified as appropriate subjects for HHFA research. The Administrator was also required to make estimates of housing need and of "progress toward meeting the need,"

and to make recommendations for legislation to make up any assumed deficiencies.

(5) A new program of loans and subsidies for farmhouse construction and repair was added to the responsibilities of the Secretary of Agriculture. This permitted loans for thirty-three years at 4 percent up to a total of $250 million for constructing or repairing dwellings or other buildings on farms deemed adequate or "potentially adequate" to sustain a family. Special grants for interest payments during the first five years of the loan term were authorized in certain cases. Other grants or loans, not to exceed $1,000 per farm, were authorized solely for repair of housing facilities on farms deemed inadequate to provide a living for a family. The Secretary of Agriculture was authorized to have special research conducted in construction techniques and plans and to provide supervision for farmers carrying out construction or repair programs with loans from the Secretary.

(6) A decennial census of housing was authorized in conjunction with each decennial census of population.

A significant innovation of the Housing Act of 1949 was the authorization for technical and economic research. In conjunction with the large measure of control inherent in the federal government's subsidy and mortgage insurance programs, the authority for technical research may well lead, for all practical purposes, to federal determination of local building codes, standards, and practices, at least for residential construction. Similar domination of city planning functions is also conceivable in administration of the slum-clearance or urban redevelopment programs. Also significant were congressional directives to the HHFA Administrator and the Secretary of Agriculture to develop housing objectives for the nation and to recommend legislation and to make reports of progress toward these goals. The assertion of federal interest and responsibility in fields previously considered to be subject to state and local jurisdiction could hardly be more positive.

Later in the session Congress adopted a proposal under which FHA was specially authorized to insure mortgages on rental housing (at 90 percent of value, 4 percent interest, for twenty-five-year periods) located on land adjoining military establishments or actually leased from the Army, Navy, or Air Force.[19] Here was a

19 Public Law 211, 81st Congress.

clear use of the insurance device to direct credit for a specialized purpose involving a special sort of risk.

Members of Congress also considered an elaborate bill referred to as "Housing Amendments of 1949." As introduced late in the congressional session, this measure[20] consolidated proposals on a variety of subjects which major bills had introduced earlier for "aids to private enterprise." The main features of this bill included:

(1) Modifications of FHA operations to provide: (a) a new system of mortgage insurance for low-priced suburban and rural houses under Title I; (b) an increase in Title II authorization and liberalized mortgage limits for the thirty-year mortgages authorized by the Housing Act of 1948; (c) provision for the separate administration in FHA of mortgage insurance for cooperative projects; (d) authority for permitting, under certain circumstances, moratoria on mortgage payments for FHA-insured mortgages; (e) an extension of Title VI rental housing mortgage insurance operations; and (f) a revision of FHA budget controls for greater flexibility in field office operations.

(2) Proposals for direct governmental lending as follows: (a) from the Veterans' Administration to qualified veterans, twenty-five-year loans at 4 percent interest; (b) from the HHFA to cooperatives, loans at 3 percent interest for sixty-year terms; (c) from the HHFA to educational institutions, loans at $2\frac{1}{2}$ percent interest for forty-year terms; (d) loans from the RFC to distributors of prefabricated houses; and (e) FHA-insured loans from the FNMA to cooperative housing associations or rental project sponsors. The first four of these classes of loans might be without any equity investment; the last class would be governed by the pertinent FHA requirements.

(3) An increase in the amount of the VA's guarantee for owner-occupant borrowers from the previous limit of 50 percent of loan or $4,000, to a new limit of 60 percent of loan or $7,500.

(4) An increase in the aggregate authorization for purchases by the FNMA of FHA-insured and VA-guaranteed loans, with virtual elimination of the existing limitation of such purchases to 50 percent of the eligible loans originated by individual mortgagees.

(5) Detailed provisions for disposition of federally-owned war housing and veterans' emergency housing as follows: (a) transfer of about 32,000 permanent units to local public housing authorities

20 S. 2246, 81st Congress.

for low-rent housing; (b) sale of about 110,000 units in other permanent projects to private investors; (c) authorization for local governments to decide, within stipulated time periods, whether temporary housing projects should be demolished or given free to the local governments involved; and (d) instructions for later federal demolition of remaining temporary housing projects.

In the House of Representatives a substitute measure was passed after extensive hearings on the above proposals.[21] All proposals for direct federal lending were omitted from this bill except a provision for loans to educational institutions, at not more than 4 percent interest for forty years, to be made by the RFC; the final decision on disposition of federally-owned war housing was deferred by a six-month extension of the existing January 1, 1950 deadline.

As the end of the first session of the Eighty-first Congress approached, it was evident that Senate passage of a companion measure and conference agreement would be unlikely before adjournment. Accordingly, final decisions were deferred until 1950 by adoption of a joint resolution[22] which (1) extended into 1950 the various existing mortgage and loan insurance programs of FHA under Section 608 and Titles I and II, (2) adopted a new basis for FHA budget determinations, (3) increased the FNMA authority for purchase of mortgage loans, with removal of the 50 percent limitation from loans guaranteed by the VA under Section 501 and from FHA-insured loans under Title VIII for military housing, and (4) extended for one year the January 1, 1950 deadline for disposition of federally-owned war housing.

Thus, Congress rejected during 1949 proposals for direct government loans to individual veterans and to cooperatives. These proposals, which were strongly supported by labor and veterans' organizations and by certain charitable associations, had as their objective the assurance that long-term loans at submarket interest rates would be available for housing for veterans and cooperative organizations. No claim was made in either case that the proposed lending schemes were economically sound or that the proposed interest rate was adequate to cover the necessary costs. A public

21 H.R. 6070, 81st Congress.
22 Senate Joint Resolution 134, 81st Congress.

interest assumed to be inherent in benefits to the favored groups was the basic justification for intervention. The sixty-year terms and 3 percent interest rate requested for cooperatives in the initial versions of the "Housing Amendments of 1949" indicated the extent to which this type of governmental intervention can be demanded.

LONG-TERM PROGRAMS OF STATES

In addition to the actions of the federal government, a number of states initiated programs of positive governmental intervention in nonfarm real estate. These programs have dealt principally, though not exclusively, with assistance to rental housing construction and with land assembly for urban redevelopment. Additional legislation, however, pertains to building codes, to special loan facilities, and to basic studies of housing conditions.

Nonemergency state legislation for local or state assistance to publicly-owned permanent housing has been enacted by five states,[23] exclusive of the authorization for local participation in the federal low-rent housing program, which has been passed by forty-two states.[24] Local or state assistance to low-rent housing has been provided for in Illinois, New Hampshire, New York, and Rhode Island, while assistance for moderate-rental housing has been authorized in Connecticut, New York, and Rhode Island. Connecticut offers to make FHA-insured loans from a state fund at low interest rates to selected families. State assistance for publicly-owned, low-rent housing is provided in the form of capital grants in Illinois, annual subsidies in New York and New Hampshire, low-interest loans in New York, and temporary financing in New Hampshire. Additional assistance from the localities involved has been authorized in the form of annual subsidies in New York City and in Woonsocket, Rhode Island, tax exemption in New Hampshire and New York, capital grants to match state funds in Illinois, and guarantee of local housing authority bonds in New York City and in Woonsocket.

[23] Not included are temporary state or local programs in seven states for building permanent housing for sale or rent to veterans. The "emergency" and "permanent" aspects of the programs are not always readily distinguishable. See Chapter 7, including footnote 19, for reference material. The "temporary" or "permanent" characteristics of the state measures are not always readily distinguishable.

[24] Enabling legislation was in effect by mid-1949 in all states except Iowa, Kansas, Oklahoma, South Dakota, Utah, and Wyoming.

In Connecticut and New York general authorizations allow
localities to provide publicly-owned housing for rentals above the
low-rent level. Rhode Island has made a similar specific authorization for the benefit of Providence. All three programs involve (1)
the use of tax-exempt bonds to minimize financing costs, (2) partial or complete tax exemption for the properties, and (3) effective guarantee of principal and interest payments on the bonds.
The guarantee in Connecticut is provided by the state; in New
York, by the city involved. In Providence, the effect of a guarantee
by the city is accomplished by having the projects financed with
municipal bonds.

When the Housing Act of 1949 authorized federal assistance to
localities in clearing slums and redeveloping blighted areas, twenty-
seven states and the District of Columbia already had statutes authorizing local activity in these fields.[25] Alabama became the twenty-
eighth state by adopting enabling legislation in August 1949. Of
the twenty-nine jurisdictions (including the District of Columbia),
thirteen authorize private companies to be formed and assist in
redevelopment projects; twelve permit local housing authorities to
perform land assembly and clearance functions; and fourteen provide for direct municipal action or public redevelopment agencies
as special agents of the localities involved. Legislation in all except
five of the states permits the redevelopment programs to take advantage of federal assistance, although in some cases adjustments
will be required to make the federal loans or grants authorized by
the Housing Act of 1949 specifically available. A common feature
of redevelopment legislation in most states is the use of eminent
domain for land acquisition either by the redevelopment body or
by the city on behalf of the redevelopment body. In some instances
acquisition of part of a redevelopment area by negotiation is required before condemnation is permitted. Tax exemption, or
restrictions for periods ranging from ten to forty years, are authorized for private redevelopers in seven states. These states, providing
for clearance by public agencies, permit city bond financing of
acquisition costs as a means of underwriting any losses incurred in
clearance and disposition. Five states authorize special taxes for
financing the net cost of clearance operations.

25 *A Handbook of Information on Provisions of the Housing Act of 1949,* Housing
and Home Finance Agency, July 1949, p. 6.

Frequently, state legislation requires that urban redevelopment be in accord with either officially approved general city plans or with publicly-approved specific plans for the project area. In Wisconsin and the District of Columbia, the redevelopment plans may establish maximum rentals for housing units provided by redevelopers. Stuyvesant Town in New York City was the first publicly-aided redevelopment project, though additional projects have been started in New York City and in Indianapolis. In July 1949 eight other cities were prepared to undertake projects and about seventy were considering projects.[26]

When public discussion of housing problems progressed, at least eleven states authorized comprehensive studies of housing problems within their states by either legislative committees or executive agencies of the government. In several instances such studies have formed the basis of new or revised legislation.

As mentioned in Chapter 6, a few states, notably California and Mississippi, have provided special funds for purchasing farms and homes to be resold to veterans, with the financing arranged by long-term debts to the state agency.

26 *Ibid.*, p. 6.

The Indirect Impacts of Government

DIRECT governmental influence, vast as it has become, does not include all phases of the state's impact on real estate financing. Numerous other means of influence exist, and, although these exert their force indirectly, they are nonetheless real and important. The area of indirect impact is, indeed, almost as broad as the whole range of legislation dealing with economic conditions. A tariff law, immigration, labor, or transport policies, a revenue measure, or any act affecting farm or urban prosperity will ultimately have some influence on real property. It is not practicable here to identify all these manifestations of government nor even to examine thoroughly the major indirect forces. But even a limited discussion of a few of them will suffice to show how the real estate market is dependent upon political action.

THE PROPERTY TAX

The property tax is one of the most important secondary influences. From a time when wealth was largely in land and chattels, and manufacture and trade were incidental, the property tax remains the main support of local government and, with a number of exceptions, a contributor to the financing of state government. Since, as the tax is administered, property has come mainly to mean real property, its incidence has a definite influence on real estate investment. In an area with high property taxes, the property tax may well amount to one-fifth or more of the gross income on an income-producing property such as rental housing. If conditions in the market do not permit the shifting of the property tax to the tenant, net income may be reduced relative to other investments, the value of the property reduced relative to other investment goods of similar cost, and hence the volume of new investment retarded. On the other hand, if the tax can be shifted the effect is to direct new investment to properties that will appeal to tenants financially able to carry the load. The property tax also has an influence on the location of residential and other structures, a drift to relatively low tax areas being inevitable where the choice of location is optional. As between comparable properties within a locality, but in different taxing jurisdictions, a difference in the current property tax tends to become capitalized into a difference in property value, so the effect of the tax is to create artificial differences in real estate investment opportunities. Even compensating differences in services rendered in high tax areas are likely to offset only to a limited degree the attraction of lower property tax rates.

Because real estate is necessarily a long-term investment offering a slow return of total capital and because, at the same time, the income from real property is highly variable, the property tax creates special hazards. The tax is relatively inflexible and, over long periods, its tendency has been to rise. Thus in bad times a property may suddenly be thrown into a deficit, while, on older properties, taxes may be borne only at the neglect of maintenance. The total influence of the property tax is not only to limit the amount and type of real estate investment but also to increase its speculative character, and to induce "milking" of property in its early years and neglect thereafter.[1]

The search for new sources of local and state revenues has been proceeding rapidly. New York City with its telephone and sales taxes and Philadelphia with its payroll tax are but two examples. Additional franchise taxes, tobacco, gasoline, and liquor taxes, and special charges for city services are other methods pursued.[2] These efforts, however, amid the constantly increasing costs of municipal government, have at best served to retard or prevent increases in the property tax. Through income taxes, general or specific sales taxes, license fees, and other means, many of the states and some municipalities have reduced their dependence for revenues on direct levies on real estate. So far, however, the basic difficulty with respect to financing local governments has hardly been met, and the uneven load on realty investment remains. The remedy offered

[1] For more detail on the impact of the property tax on realty investment, see Miles L. Colean, *American Housing* (The Twentieth Century Fund, New York, 1944) pp. 236 ff. See also, Carl Shoup, Roy Blough, and Mabel Newcomer, *Facing the Tax Problem* (The Twentieth Century Fund, New York, 1937) pp. 10 ff.; Harold M. Groves, *Postwar Taxation and Economic Progress* (New York, 1946) pp. 344 ff.

[2] Urban Land Institute, *News and Trends in City Development*, Vol. 5, No. 4 (April 1946).

by the limitations on the property tax, which are a feature of some state constitutions, are only a partial remedy. They set bounds to the amount of the load but do not solve the problem of inequality.

THE INCOME TAX

The income tax creates additional problems for corporate-owned real estate. Applied to an investment that already is carrying a large share of the total cost of local government, the corporate income tax further reduces a relatively thin margin of net income.[3] For real-estate-owning corporations, the only escape is through the creation and maintenance of a high proportion of debt, since interest payments are deductible in the tax calculation. In this case the result is to induce dependence on mortgage rather than on equity financing and even to encourage disguising, as some form of fixed debt, that which would normally be equity financing.

Another hazard is created by the incompatibility of the tax system with the repayment of mortgage debt, since amortization payments are made from net income and are not deductible for tax purposes. The situation creates an incentive either to maintain a high fixed debt or to substitute for it an arrangement involving a sale of property and taking back under a long-term lease with fixed rental payments (which are deductible). The latter device, applied mainly to industrial and store properties, has been a feature of insurance company investment since the war.[4] The difficulty created by the corporate income tax system is especially sharp in connection with loans having a fixed regular payment compounded of decreasing interest and increasing amortization shares, such as is characteristic of most insured mortgage loans on rental property. The interest portion is deductible from income in calculating taxable net income; the amortization portion, on the other hand, is not deductible. The depreciation allowance is deductible and this may exceed amortization, but, whereas amortization requirements increase under the level payment plan, depreciation allowances are fixed, and when the former equal the latter (usually

3 According to U. S. Treasury, *Statistics of Income,* Part 2, 1938-42, the net return to urban real estate corporations, figured on its relation either to total invested capital or to equity capital, was lower than for any other form of corporate enterprise. It is probable that this unfavorable dividend status for real estate corporations is at least partly offset by heavier salary payments to owner-officers of these corporations.

4 See Chapter 4.

at an early point in the life of an individual investment) the mortgagor is required to pay an increased income tax and to continue to disburse cash to meet amortization and interest requirements. This may be a very heavy burden on the cash resources of the owner, and, under some circumstances, might be serious enough to cause a default. The net effect is to induce the equity holder to be more concerned with the quick recoupment of a minimum equity than with considerations of long-term investment. The tax system thus aggravates the speculative character of the equity investment and, in doing so, adds to the risk of the mortgagee.[5]

In respect to owner-occupied housing, the interest payment deduction allowed under the personal income tax is often looked upon as a special benefit to the homeowner. But it is a benefit only as long as he remains in debt. Consequently, there is a lessened incentive to repayment of debt in order to maintain a maximum income tax benefit. Another income tax advantage to the homeowner, which indirectly influences housing investments, is the exclusion from gross income of any amount for the rental value of owner-occupied homes.

TAX EXEMPTION

Both the property and income tax systems contain exemptions or abatements that give special advantages to certain types of investment or investing institutions. Thus, public housing developments are generally relieved of any substantial contribution to the maintenance of the municipalities in which they are located. New York and Massachusetts, for instance, provide for less-than-normal taxes for property developed and operated under their urban redevelopment statutes. Tax concessions on industrial property are widespread,[6] and a number of the states have laws exempting

[5] For a fuller treatment of the investment problems raised by the corporate income tax, with particular reference to the "constant payment" plan of mortgage financing, see Randolph E. Paul and Miles L. Colean, *Effect of the Corporate Income Tax on Investment in Rental Housing* (National Committee on Housing, Inc., New York, 1946). Also to be noted is the fact that the capital gains feature of our income tax is biased in favor of investment in securities as against investment in real estate. A man who buys and sells real estate is more readily regarded as a dealer than is a securities trader and his gains are taxed as ordinary income rather than as capital gains (H. M. Groves, *op. cit.*).

[6] H. M. Groves, *op. cit.*, pp. 341-43.

homesteads from all or part of the property tax.[7] Federally-owned
property is not subject to state or local taxation. And religious and
eleemosynary institutions receive substantial tax concessions in
many states.

Designed as incentives to certain types of investment and as a
special protection to others, all such concessions add to the inequal-
ities already existing in property tax assessments; and, even more
important, they inevitably increase the burden on the remainder
of real property excluded from the benefits. While by no means a
general rule, the tendency is to favor industrial property, owner-
occupied dwellings, and "social purpose" housing to the corresponding disadvantage of investment in income-producing property
of commercial and conventional residential types.

Income tax exemptions are also significant in the realty investment picture, since certain types of mortgage lending institutions
obtain a competitive advantage both as to the interest rates that
may be charged and the income that may be returned. Thus, national farm loan associations, federal savings and loan associations,
state-chartered savings and loan associations, and mutual savings
banks enjoy immunities under the federal income tax laws and in
general are also given favored treatment under state and local tax
laws. National banks and state commercial banks are not thus
privileged. Life insurance companies, by special arrangement, are
taxed only for the amount of income in excess of that allocable to
legal reserves, with the result that the incidence of the tax on total
income is minor.[8] Government corporations and agencies (federal,
state, and local) engaged in realty financing pay no income taxes, a
circumstance which, combined with the low interest at which
they can obtain their funds, gives them a strong advantage if their
activities become competitive with unprivileged private institutions.

THE PROBLEM OF MUNICIPAL ORGANIZATION

Adding to the difficulties created by the property tax is the problem created by the organization of our municipalities and metro-

[7] See Chapter 3.
[8] The minor burden of income taxes on insurance companies makes it advantageous for these institutions to invest in income-producing properties suitable for
long-term lease to substantial tenants. In such cases, the tenants avoid income taxes
on the rental paid and the investing insurance company also has the advantage of
comparative tax immunity.

politan districts. As the demand for additional services from government has grown, the tendency has often been to set up independent taxing authorities to provide the services. Thus, we have not only an overlapping of state, county, and municipal levies on property, but often a congeries of levies from school, park, and sanitary districts, special assessment areas, and others, all independently computed, but all placed against the same property. Rarely is there a single authority to correlate the claims of all agencies in terms of their relative importance and with due regard for the ability of property owners to pay.

Even more far reaching in its effect on urban realty investment is the independent jurisdiction of satellite communities. In most metropolitan areas the central city is prevented from extending its limits by the suburban communities that surround it. The satellites depend on the central city for their existence and profit from the services it provides; yet they are free from the burden of its support. At the same time the movement of industry and population to outlying sections deprives the central city of revenue. The result is an increasing burden of taxes on centrally located properties, a decrease in their ability to pay (and consequently in their value), and discouragement of new investment in core areas. On the other hand, lower taxes and frequently more lenient building regulations tend to cause new real estate investment to follow population to the suburban regions.

Various attempts have been made to compensate for this situation. New York led the way with its Redevelopment Companies Acts of 1942 and 1943, which provided that taxes on housing properties built in reclaimed areas might be frozen for twenty-five years at the level existing before redevelopment.[9] This measure has an effect on the financial structure of a housing investment more than equivalent to the complete writing off of land value during the period of the abatement. Massachusetts offered a more complex but less beneficial plan of the same nature.[10] Legislation with a similar purpose had, by September 1, 1949, been passed in twenty-seven states and the District of Columbia.[11] Indiana, for instance, authorized Indianapolis to levy a special realty tax to furnish funds

[9] New York Laws c. 845 (1942); New York Laws c. 234 (1943).
[10] Acts and Resolves of Massachusetts c. 654 (1945).
[11] Data from Urban Land Institute, Washington. See also Chapter 8.

for the purchase of blighted urban areas, and empowered the redevelopment authority to resell the land at prices compatible with
its earning power when redeveloped.[12] Illinois provided for outright state and municipal grants to support these functions.[13] The
federal Housing Act of 1949 supplements state and local funds for
redevelopment activity.[14]

Such efforts to induce private investment in central areas are
usually accompanied by some extension of governmental control
over management. Generally, a requirement is made that the re-use
be in keeping with approved redevelopment plans or general city
plans. Among the more common controls established are those that
regulate the capital structure and restrict rental charges and return
on the investment. The regulation may, directly or indirectly, affect
the physical character of the development, methods of operation,
and selection of tenants.

INFLUENCE OF FISCAL POLICIES

Because of the direct bearing of municipal, and often of state, expenditures on the tax load carried by real property, the fiscal policies of these authorities obviously have a very considerable effect
upon the returns from realty investment. The fiscal and monetary
policies of the federal government, while perhaps less direct, may
be more profound in their influence. For example, the need for
intervention to save mortgagors from economic catastrophe in the
panic of 1837 can be traced closely to the loose credit and monetary
practices of the 1830's followed by the suddenly instituted hard
money policy of the federal government.[15] Other periods of strain
on the mortgage credit system need thorough study to determine
the extent of their relationships to the general monetary situation.
The present time is a case in point.

The increase in the public debt following fifteen years of depression and war (1930-45) naturally caused the federal government to be much concerned not only with the sale of its bonds but
also with the bond interest rate. The heavy dependence placed by

12 Indiana Laws c. 276 (1945).
13 Illinois Senate Bills 39 and 201, Session of 1945.
14 Public Law 171, 81st Congress; Chapter 8.
15 See Ray Allen Billington, *Westward Expansion* (New York, 1949) pp. 364-68.

the Treasury on the banking system for absorption of successive issues (resulting in an increase in the money supply) and the low interest rate policy maintained throughout this period had two effects on real estate investment. One was to contribute to the inflation of capital values, already stimulated by a short supply of residential and commercial structures during and after the war; the other was to create a downward pressure on the mortgage interest rate.

During 1947 and 1948, fear of further inflation caused some modification in Treasury policy, which tended both to reduce the amount of debt held by the banks and to relieve some of the pressure on interest rates. Demands for new industrial loans added to the upward movement of rates. These influences were reflected in some tightening in mortgage credit. Although the new trend was welcomed in some quarters for its presumed counterinflationary effect, it faced opposition in other directions as endangering the expansion of residential construction and as increasing the federal burden of debt financing.

Up to this time, the policy of direct pressure on the mortgage interest rate (through the Federal Housing Administration and the Veterans' Administration) as a means for increasing the housing supply had harmonized with, and benefited from, the general fiscal policy. The modification of fiscal policy thus created a new realm of conflict and gave impetus to proposals to fix mortgage interest rates independently of fluctuations of rates in the financial markets and indeed of the broader governmental attitude on credit expansion. However, by mid-1949 general fiscal policy of the government, as well as housing policy, again favored low interest rates.

It should be noted that the stress on the maintenance of low interest rates on mortgage loans threatens to remove one means of effecting market readjustments. If rates are kept at low levels during an inflationary period, further reductions to provide a stimulus in any subsequent period of deflation become difficult or impossible except in combination with a government subsidy. A settled policy of low mortgage interest rates would thus point to an expansion of governmental controls to compensate for the weakening of automatic market adjustments.

PUBLIC WORKS

Public works affect real estate investment by their cost, location, and timing. The majority of community projects are financed either from special assessments or from general property tax funds; in either case the cost is carried by the owners of real estate. A community which, in spite of high tax charges, carries out well-devised programs of public improvement is likely, within limits, to have an investment advantage over a community where a low tax rate is combined with inadequate services. However, the possibility of excessive burdens from such expenditures is one of the hazards of realty investment.

The building of a bridge, tunnel, or rapid transit extension may open a dormant urban area to investment. Such improvements may also drain value from older areas. In Chicago, for instance, the subdivision boom of the 1920's resulted mainly from a series of actual or projected transit extensions. Streets, schools, and parks all play a vital part in determining the point and profitability of investment. The power of public works to contribute to, or detract from, the investment potentials of an area is thus exceedingly great.[16]

Real estate investment is also affected by the timing of public works in so far as the coincidence of high public and private activity aggravates a construction boom. Traditional methods of financing and public demand both for necessary extensions of community services, such as water and sewer facilities, and for additional improvements in times of prosperity and high building activity tend to concentrate locally financed public works in periods of prosperity. Public construction under such circumstances becomes directly competitive with private investment for short supplies of labor and materials and so contributes to higher costs and nonmaintainable levels of property values. On the other hand, state and local public works, which ordinarily constitute the bulk of the total, tend to be sharply reduced during the early stages of a contraction. Thus, customary public works policies not only tend to increase costs during expansions but also tend to add to defla-

16 See Herbert D. Simpson, "The Influence of Public Improvements on Real Estate Values," *Annals of the American Academy of Political and Social Science,* Vol. 148, March 1930, for a review of a case in which the supposed benefits to specific property owners from a public works program were badly miscalculated.

tionary pressures during contractions.[17] Actually, therefore, they must be looked upon as important contributors to the instability of realty values and to the hazards of real estate investment.

SECURITY LEGISLATION

A new type of impact on real estate investment is developing from a wide range of state and federal social security measures, such as old age and health benefits, unemployment insurance, minimum wage laws, parity prices, subsidies for production or nonproduction, crop insurance, and so forth. This source of impact on realty investment is too complex for analysis in this study, yet it warrants brief consideration.

All of these measures affect the level and continuity of private income. Those affecting agriculture directly influence farm income and hence will tend to be reflected in farm real estate prices, while security benefits for urban workers may help to determine the rents and prices that may be afforded for urban houses, modifying in some degree the trend of investment. To the extent that such benefits are constant, or increasing in value, they may tend to give an element of stability to real estate finance and to improve the opportunity for investment. To the extent, however, that the payments are of limited or of limitable duration, the results may be to the contrary.

GOVERNMENTAL RESEARCH ACTIVITIES

The technical and economic research carried on by governmental agencies has had, and promises increasingly to have, profound influences on realty investment. Early in the thirties, following the leadership of Cleveland, the first "real property inventories" appeared. Prior to that time, land-use maps had been prepared in a number of places, but the inventories disclosed, for the first time, organized facts regarding the type, size, condition, age, and rental of urban dwellings. Financed with relief funds and carried out under the direction first of the Department of Commerce and later of the Works Progress Administration, these surveys were conducted in a large number of cities. Some of the inventories were

---

17 For a discussion of the difficulties involved in expanding public works during depression periods, see Miles L. Colean, *Stabilizing the Construction Industry* (National Planning Association, Washington, 1945).

supplemented by the "Financial Survey of Urban Housing" (also financed as a relief project) which provided information not hitherto available on values, rents, debt and debt delinquency, type of tenure, and similar data for sixty-one cities or metropolitan areas.

The Home Loan Bank Board and the FHA undertook a considerable amount of research useful to investors and mortgage lenders. All this led up to the general Housing Census of 1940, in which comprehensive data on the nation's housing supply were brought together. Related to these data are the building permit figures of the Bureau of Labor Statistics (Department of Labor), the construction estimates of the Construction Division (Office of Domestic Commerce, Department of Commerce), the population and business data of the Bureau of the Census (Department of Commerce), and other material collected by a number of federal agencies. There remain, however, many serious gaps in the economic data needed by realty investors to formulate sound judgments.[18]

In 1935, the Division of Economics and Statistics of the FHA listed the following series as essential in the field of housing: rents, occupancy and vacancy, building operating expenses, real estate values, real estate transfers, subdividing activity, new construction, construction costs, mortgage recordings, foreclosures, real estate taxes and delinquencies and population data (growth, shifts, marriages, etc.). At that time, current information on only a few of these subjects was available and most of that was inadequate. Yet the inadequacies of the data on housing were as nothing compared to those on other types of real estate. During World War II, the Census, by the use of sampling techniques, contributed greatly to current knowledge, particularly of congested centers. But the effort was scattered and sporadic and no means have been provided for its continuance. Fourteen years after the FHA report referred to above, the situation was much the same. The Housing Act of 1948, passed during the special session of the Eightieth Congress, authorized the Housing and Home Finance Agency to conduct technical research to promote standardized building codes and standardized dimensions for building materials. In the Housing Act of 1949, this authorization to the Housing and Home Finance

18 Many of the existing series are subject to grave shortcomings. See *Report of the Conference on Housing Statistics,* Housing and Home Finance Agency, January-March 1947.

Agency was extended to permit a broad range of technical and economic research in the field of housing.[19]

In the past, construction (much the same sort of small local business as agriculture) has received little from the government for technological research compared with the scientific and developmental work done for agriculture. During the twenties the Department of Commerce made a beginning in this field. Programs were instituted for simplifying the variety of manufactured products and processes, for model building codes, planning laws, zoning ordinances, mechanic's lien laws, and for making tests necessary to substantiate code requirements.

Modest as this endeavor was, and fruitful as it promised to be, nearly all the activities mentioned were drastically curtailed in 1933, just at the time when the government was assuming a major part of the risk and direction of farm and residential mortgage activity. Since that time, in spite of meager appropriations, the Forest Products Laboratory of the Department of Agriculture has done notable original research beneficial to construction, particularly in the development and use of plywood,[20] while the National Bureau of Standards of the Department of Commerce has carried on simplification and construction standards programs and a much limited testing program.

War and postwar pressures disclosed the desirability of a more advanced technology of construction, particularly housing construction. Emergency funds were allocated to the War Production Board and the National Housing Agency for specific research projects. After the end of hostilities the technical research functions of the War Production Board were transferred to an Office of Technical Services in the Department of Commerce, where, during 1945 and 1946, a relatively small allocation was made for research in construction methods.

This chapter has tried to suggest, without attempting to be inclusive, the ramifications of indirect governmental influences on realty finance. It is clear that the impacts are numerous and that their effects are substantial; certainly remoteness is no criterion of their consequence. For example, there are many influences on real

[19] See Chapter 8.
[20] The main impetus to prefabricated house construction in the prewar period came from this activity.

estate finance resulting from the numerous impacts of government
upon the construction industry through such matters as local licensing laws for contractors, engineers, architects, and artisans (which
in some cases serve to enforce local restrictive practices and hence
to raise costs), the federal antitrust laws (which are designed to
maintain competition and hence to keep costs down), the relatively
weak state antimonopoly legislation (which fails to prevent local
restraints beyond federal reach), and the broad immunity of labor
organizations from federal antitrust action. While it is clear that
these conditions are significant elements of the essentially political
environment in which real estate financing operations are carried
on, their ramifications are too complex to be described satisfactorily
in a study of this scope.

Summary: The Environment
of Real Estate Finance

ALTHOUGH the existing influence of government on real estate finance in the United States is for the most part the product of a few decades, the encompassing measures of the 1930's and 1940's were not strictly the inventions of that short period. Instead, as it has been the purpose of this study to point out, they were the outgrowth of a long period of mounting tensions, which, in turn, were largely the product of earlier attitudes toward government and earlier expressions of governmental power.

Although the initial course of real estate development in this country was marked by resistance to all forms of social and economic control, the force of government, as a means for advancing popular objectives, was not neglected. The wilderness was a great absorber of capital, and continuous public and private efforts were pursued to make the capital available. State credit was used lavishly for public improvements, and large sections of the federal domain were donated for the same purpose. The desire to attract private capital was reflected in the first era of settlement and expansion by simplifying foreclosure, strengthening the lender's remedies, and regularizing transfer procedures as compared with English precedents. It continued to be reflected in numerous early land bank schemes and, later, in the immersion, directly and indirectly, of state-chartered commercial banks in real estate finance. In this period demands for easy mortgage credit were initiated that have persisted to the present day.[1]

GROWTH OF CONFLICT

The combination of diffused, small ownership, overexpansion, excessive speculation, and heavy borrowing gave inherent weaknesses

[1] Charles J. Bullock (*Essays on the Monetary History of the United States*, New York, 1900, p. 1) states: ". . . a strong movement for cheap money has existed continuously in this country from the earliest period of colonization."

to both urban and rural real estate investment. At times the risks accepted by borrowers became intolerable. The favored methods of amelioration were the granting of temporary relief from debt payment and the modification of the mortgage laws to give increased protection to borrowers—as, for example, successive moratoria from the panic of 1820 onward, as well as the tendency to increase redemption periods, which appeared at about that time.[2]

The risks were hardly less painful to savers than to lenders, as the repeated waves of bank failures testify, and an assurance of future safety was sought by limiting the freedom of lending institutions to make real estate loans. To the extent that these limitations were effective—and, for the most part, they tended to be so immediately after a severe liquidation—they served to lessen the availability of mortgage funds. At the same time the easing of the mortgage contract in favor of the borrower increased the risk to the lender and hence tended to raise interest rates. The net result of the palliatives was to make mortgage money scarce or dear, or both; in other words, to run squarely in face of the demand for easy credit. The situation was, of course, complicated by the cumbersomeness of legal structure and the apparent unwillingness of the states to maintain the flexibility and adaptability that often characterized early legislation.

The conflict in policy thus engendered found no resolution; and indeed it was incapable of satisfactory resolution so long as borrowers insisted on maintaining their hard-won protections and lending institutions were subjected to rigid limitations on their lending activities. The stage was set for some special intercession that would promise both cheap and plentiful credit and that would still protect the participants from catastrophe. The federal government alone could produce such a prodigy.

And further, as good farm lands were taken up and cities became congested and far-flung, new problems impinging on real estate investment developed. In order to bring an end to, or at least to moderate, the overexploitation of land to the detriment of physical and human resources, state and national governments sought to strengthen their means of control. Conservation became a rallying

[2] Robert H. Skilton, *Government and the Mortgage Debtor* (Philadelphia, 1944) pp. 28-34, shows the dates in which the redemption statutes were enacted in the several states.

cry; building codes were amplified, and zoning codes and other means of regulating urban land improvement, buildings, and occupancy were widely adopted. Under broadened interpretations, economic as well as physical considerations were included within the purview of the police power, and zoning was expanded to cover rural as well as urban areas. Land planning gradually became a governmental function, claiming broad power over methods of land use and hence over the environment and substance of real estate investment.

Because of the dependence of most of these new forms of intervention on the police power, they first appeared, for the most part, through state and municipal action. Excepting for the federal government's diminishing land transactions, its flood control activity, and a tentative approach to conservation and reclamation, the power of intervention was not sought. Nevertheless, it became gradually evident that the problems of settling arid lands, of protecting national resources, of bolstering the farm economy, and of restoring rural and urban districts would not, or could not, be solved by the types of measures already devised. And, to a steadily increasing number of people, the federal government alone appeared to have the power necessary to achieve these large objectives. It was not, however, until after World War I, and, more particularly, until the 1930's, that the pressure for federal action appeared in any large measure and that the constitutional means for effectuating it were discovered.

SHIFT TO FEDERAL DOMINANCE

The first resort to federal authority directly affecting real estate finance grew out of mounting demands for specialized farm credit facilities and resulted in the creation of the Federal Land Bank System in 1916. When this system met the test of constitutionality, the pattern for much future federal intervention was set. Devices of one sort or another to extend or facilitate real estate credit became the principal means of satisfying the demands for federal aid following the mortgage crisis of the 1930's.

The credit authority, however, was not the only means of federal intervention. The power over inland waterways was expanded to permit comprehensive planning schemes such as the Tennessee Valley Authority; the power of eminent domain was invoked in the advancement of public housing; and under World War II emergency powers the scope of the government's influence on realty investment was again greatly expanded through limitations on construction, rents, the sale of new residential properties, and lending activity.

In the resurgence of intervention there was a marked emphasis on the concept of control for the sake of protecting the welfare of the individual, a point of view in marked contrast to that which characterized governmental action in the nineteenth century. Broadly speaking, the main aim of government land policy during the period of national expansion was to encourage enterprise rather than to provide it with physical or economic protection. An individual's welfare, from this viewpoint, rested mainly on the vigor of his own initiative rather than on state aid or support.

In the past, stays of foreclosure were exceptions, and these were always temporary and aimed at restoring the functioning of enterprise and initiative. Another exception was the development of governmental supervision of financial institutions. In this case both the consideration of welfare (that of depositors, shareholders, and the like) and the substitution of governmental restraint and direction (over the investment policies of the institutions) were present. Despite these exceptions, it is still broadly true that until the thirties the main and continuous objective of government (both federal and state) was to encourage real estate as a form of enterprise. Secondary efforts (left almost wholly to the states) were concerned with the temporary support or restoration of enterprise when it was in danger.

With the establishment of the Federal Land Bank System, however, a modification in the government approach became evident. This agency was designed to make credit available under terms and conditions which did not then exist in the private financial market. There was the same point of view in creating the Federal Home Loan Bank System, and it was pursued further in establishing the Federal Housing Administration for the purpose of influencing the specialized use of credit to finance certain classes of housing. As this last-named agency developed, specialization became more definite: certain classes of housing received greater aid than others (single family houses below a set value, cooperatives, nonprofit corporations, etc.); certain classes of borrowers (first, war workers, then veterans, then families of "moderate" or "lower" income) received benefits not available to others. The device, moreover, was used to accomplish ends not strictly germane to the credit transaction, such as the improvement of housing standards, the influencing of land planning, and the regulation of wages paid to construction workers.

During this evolution, the government has become a guardian of individual welfare, exercising an enlarged influence on private decisions and taking greater responsibility for results. The movement is even more clearly evident in the resettlement and tenant-purchase activities of the Farm Security Administration (later the Farmers' Home Administration) and in the subsidized housing activities of the Public Housing Administration and its ancillary local authorities. It was evident also in the continued regulation of rents, in enforcing priorities for veterans in newly built houses, and in the special provisions for maintaining a fixed interest rate for loans to veterans following World War II.

EXTENT OF CONTROL

Out of this development, in which practically every source of governmental power has been invoked, real estate activity and its financing emerge more fully subject to governmental influence, regulation, and control than any part of the economy not distinctly of a public or public utility character. A review of the controls now existing and of the means by which they were brought about will illustrate this conclusion.

The power of the state as the original owner of the land has been asserted in the planning and use of land still in its ownership or reacquired through tax delinquency and purchase. In the re-acquisition of land, the power of eminent domain, employed under new and broadened definitions of public purpose, has been a powerful instrument in both local and federal hands. It has permitted local governments not only to provide land for thoroughfares, parks, public buildings, and public utilities, but to remove land for public housing and redevelopment purposes from private ownership, and by so doing to bring about major alterations in the structure of cities. Thus the government goes beyond the mere reassembly of land to support numerous projects in social and economic planning.

In the federal jurisdiction, the power of eminent domain is becoming steadily more important as a means of exercising control over forest and grazing lands, certain mineral deposits, and for carrying through such comprehensive undertakings as the Tennessee Valley Authority. When constitutional limitations impeded the use of the condemnation power, jurisdiction has frequently been obtained (as with TVA) through an interpretation of the federal power to regulate interstate commerce, and, on some occasions (as in the divesting of huge acreages of private farm land for permanent or temporary military purposes), by invoking the emergency power.

The police power has developed to a degree surpassing even that of the power of eminent domain. It now appears in a vast body of state, county, and municipal laws affecting such aspects of real estate investment as the construction of buildings (building codes, sanitary codes, electrical codes, fire regulations), the occupancy and use of buildings (housing codes, sanitary codes, smoke control ordinances, closing and demolition ordinances), and the use of urban and rural land (zoning codes, subdivision regulations, planning restrictions, etc.).

The original ideas about nuisance abatement and the protection of public health and safety have been enlarged to cover matters relating to the general moral and economic welfare of the community. As they are now applied, particularly in cities, but also to a steadily increasing extent in rural areas, nearly all improvement and use of real property are subject to regulation—and there is no evidence that this development has stopped. Greater limitations on the occupancy of housing and more drastic requirements for modernization and demolition, for instance, are possible; less regard may be given in the future to the rights of nonconforming uses under zoning regulations; and planning regulations may go beyond social and economic to esthetic considerations.

The police power, combined with the chartering power, has provided the means for establishing and regulating financial institutions. Through the banking and insurance laws, the types of loans and other investments, as well as the volume of funds that can be made available for real estate investment, are regulated. The decisions of financial institutions are limited not only by the stipulations of the law but also by the attitudes and instructions of examining officials. Moreover, the law of real property, with its complex ritual of transfer and mortgage, adds another strong influence on the flow of institutional funds.

The indirect and passive effects of the taxing power on real estate investment are, of course, manifold. In addition, the taxing power has been directly used as a means of influencing investment. Inducements for investment in industrial property have been offered for many years through a decrease or elimination of the real estate tax for a period of years. The extension of the homestead exemption principle to limit property taxation, and the use of tax exemption and tax limitations, have been employed to encourage home ownership, to induce investment in rental housing property, and to stimulate slum clearance and rebuilding by private investors.

During World War II, special depreciation allowances were permitted under the federal corporate income tax in order to induce private investment for war production. Since the war, suggestions have been made for using a similar method for real estate corporations in order to encourage investment in rental housing. Another form of tax exemption has appeared in the financing of public housing projects by the issuance of the bonds of local housing authorities. Because these are authorities emanating from local government, the interest on their obligations is exempt from federal taxation. This fact, combined with a virtual guarantee of principal and interest, has resulted in a much lower interest rate than is available for other real estate financing.

The power to act in the general welfare and the power to spend in support of welfare measures have been the sources of numerous impacts, both direct and indirect, on the real estate market. Subsidies for public housing and slum clearance, for instance, have been defended on these grounds, as have the extensive measures to support the prices of farm products and hence the value of farm land.

The powers discussed above have been long recognized. Out of World War I, the depression, and World War II, however, has come a new assertion of power, departing from both the legal heritage and the former definition of constitutional limitations of the federal government. The new source of power is that created by Congress, or assumed by the President, on the grounds of "national emergency." During World War I, emergency powers (as regards real estate activity) were invoked to curtail construction, to grant priorities in the use of building materials, and to engage directly in industrial and residential building. The declaration of a national emergency during the thirties gave support to the innovations of that period. For instance, the ease with which such measures as the National Housing Act and the United States Housing Act escaped serious constitutional challenge, as compared with the much less novel Land Bank Act of a few years before, indicated the new force which that crisis brought to the interventionary trend.

With the sweeping assertion of emergency power occasioned by World War II, real estate investment was again affected. The control of construction operations through priorities and limitation orders; the control of rents, sales prices on newly built houses, prices of building materials, wages of construction workers, and the price of certain building operations; the financing of industrial construction and the direct building of emergency housing; the creation of the National Housing Agency and the temporary abolition of the Home Loan Bank Board, all resulted from extraordinary wartime powers. The same powers, in force after hostilities ceased, permitted the continuance of rent control, the limitation of construction, the issuance of priorities, and the range of activity authorized by the Veterans' Emergency Housing Act of 1946.

Although the specific measures enacted under emergency conditions have usually been of limited duration,[3] the right to invoke emergency power to meet new crises may now be considered a settled interventionary principle.

To the powers thus far discussed must be added the right to exert control directly over real estate credit. This stems mainly from broad interpretations of the monetary power delegated to the federal government by the Constitution. In nearly every respect, particularly in the federal sphere, the power to influence credit has in the long run surpassed the importance of other powers. Constitutional limitations prevent the federal government from using the police power except where interstate commerce is involved (a

[3] This has not been true in every case; for instance, the Trading with the Enemy Act of October 6, 1917 (50 App. U.S.C. § 5 (b) [1946]), which was never repealed, provided the basis for the emergency power assumed by the President in closing the banks in 1933, and for many of the executive orders prior to, and during, World War II.

rare occurrence in real estate activity); the power of eminent domain has been restricted to taking land essential for public buildings, control of navigation, and the national defense.[4] The federal
government is no longer important as a landholder, except in a few
states; and the federal taxing power has limited application as a
means of influencing realty investment. Credit, therefore, is the
main avenue of federal influence and with the shift of emphasis
from state to federal jurisdiction it has come to be the most direct
means of governmental impact on the realty market.

Credit as an All-Purpose Instrument

The federal government has used its power to influence lending
activity and to accomplish a number of objectives not all directly
related to credit conditions. A number of examples may be given.
First, the credit instrument has been used to grant privileges to special groups. Initially, privileges were extended only to borrowers
in distress [5] but now, under the Bankhead-Jones Act and the Cooley
Act (Farmers' Home Administration), they include loans for farm
purchase and improvement by tenant farmers, sharecroppers, and
owners of submarginal farms, as well as loans for the benefit of low-
income urban families under the United States Housing Act. The
same principle was used to provide for war workers and later for
veterans, under amendments to the National Housing Act and
through the Servicemen's Readjustment Act.

In extending credit to special groups two important principles
are apparent: (1) credit is made available in accordance with a
measure of need rather than a measure of risk; and (2) the terms of
credit are such as to meet the need. The objective of protecting
certain groups from the risks they have incurred has always been
present in times of distress, but there is a tendency now to embody
protective measures in the original credit instrument. For example,
there is the ease with which debt obligations may, on the occasion

4 The control over navigation (under the interstate commerce clause), as previously
noted, has been sufficient to permit an extensive use of the power to effectuate general planning schemes. The right to exercise the power of eminent domain in the
interests of national defense seems likely to expand further with the development of
atomic energy. In the general field of real estate activity, however, the federal use
of eminent domain is still negligible.

5 Through the Home Owners' Loan Corporation and the Federal Farm Mortgage
Corporation.

of distress, be modified under the Bankhead-Jones procedure and under the Servicemen's Readjustment Act for loans to veterans.[6]

Second, mortgage credit has been used to influence the type of tenure. Thus, special credit devices have been aimed at the encouragement of the family-operated farm. In cities they have been directed at the expansion of individual home ownership, and under some circumstances at the erection of rental housing.

Third, not only tenure but the character of the property has been subject to influence through the credit mechanism. Under Bankhead-Jones loans, the government maintains a measure of control over farm size and management, while under Federal Housing Administration procedure the mortgaged property is required to meet prescribed standards of location, planning, and construction. In many respects, FHA standards have provided a means of overcoming the inability of the federal government to exercise the police power directly. Land selection, land planning, building design, and construction of public housing projects are, of course, subject to almost complete control by the federal government through its loans and subsidies to public housing authorities, and a strong measure of such control will follow the loans and grants to cities for redevelopment purposes.

Fourth, the federal government influences real estate prices through FHA and Veterans' Administration appraisals and limitations on loan amount. It also controls the prices veteran borrowers are permitted to pay for their houses and the rents at which apartment properties subject to FHA-insured financing and public housing properties can be offered and assumes considerable jurisdiction over operating policies in respect to these properties. Through loans to cities for redevelopment purposes it has the final voice in setting the price at which the assembled lands are offered for re-use.

Fifth, credit devices have been used to influence many aspects of construction, such as the encouragement given to large merchant builders by the FHA system, the special appeal offered to the large contract builder by public housing, and the aid extended to manu-

---

[6] The provision for veterans' loans referred to is in § 506 of the Servicemen's Readjustment Act, 59 Stat. 626 (1944). This permits the Administrator of Veterans' Affairs, on notification of default, to pay the holder of the obligation the unpaid balance of the loan plus accrued interest and to take an assignment of the loan and security, thus allowing the Administrator to make any modified arrangement for payment that he may deem advisable.

facturers of prefabricated housing by direct loans from the Reconstruction Finance Corporation. Federal Housing Administration standards influence the whole technology of the construction industry, while the greater means of control exercised over public housing contracts and other direct loan operations, such as loans to farmers, have a similar but even more far-reaching effect.

Finally, the extension of mortgage credit has been used as an instrument for increasing employment. Closely allied was the objective of establishing a "fair" wage. Thus, where public credit was used directly, as in public works and public housing, construction wages have been set at what the Secretary of Labor found to be the "prevailing wage" in the area. Where government operates more indirectly, as in FHA-insured financing of rental housing construction, the same procedure has been applied, and a recurring effort has been made to apply it to all FHA insurance activity.

These new objectives in the use of the credit power have carried it far from its original status. The increase in availability of mortgage funds is no longer the single end; indeed, it may be overshadowed by numerous other objectives. In its new function, credit plays an integral part in a general welfare program under which government assumes responsibility for better standards of income, health, and shelter.

Persistence of Conflict

The relationship between government and real estate finance has not developed in the direction of greater simplicity or uniformity. Starting with a legal system of great complexity and a multitude of jurisdictions (from the forty-eight states to the thousands of counties, municipalities, and taxing authorities), the number of agencies with which investors must deal, and the number of matters about which they must be concerned, have grown with the years. Amid the increasing diversity of governmental powers many old conflicts have persisted and new ones have appeared. Conflicts, of course, are inevitable as long as interests differ; and the making of working compromises between interests is the basis of all law. The conflicts, however, do not arise merely from differences among the interests in an otherwise private transaction but also in different sets of governmental jurisdictions, among contrary attitudes of the function of government, and among the very objectives that government undertakes to achieve. No resolution of these conflicts has yet been accomplished.

So far, the conflict between state and local law, on the one hand, and federal initiative, on the other, has found no solution except by the federal government's reaching over state jurisdiction by insuring and guaranteeing mortgage loans, chartering specialized lending institutions, and making direct loans and subsidies. These means have served not only to draw under federal influence a large part of farm and residential finance but also to give the federal government influence on matters of land development and building that otherwise would be subject only to the police power of the states.

The second realm of conflict—that between the concept of government as an arbiter in an economic system where activity springs mainly from private decisions and the concept of government as a prime mover and director of economic activity—has so far come even less near to a working compromise. Perhaps one reason for this failure is the fact that the character of the conflict itself has not even now been clearly defined.

In its relationships with mortgage credit, government has not been guided by any consciously stated principle; intervention has been largely a matter of expediency rather than principle. As often shown in the course of this study, it has come in response to a crisis; and the nature of the crisis, rather than some basic concept of the function of government, has determined the nature of the action taken.

In most early instances of intervention, the government's role was that of a salvaging or corrective agent, and not of a permanent directive force; and it tended to withdraw soon after the immediate danger was past. This was true, for instance, of state action in staying foreclosure proceedings during financial panics. In the federal sphere, it was true of the Home Owners' Loan Corporation and the Federal Farm Mortgage Corporation. However, many crisis-bred measures, such as the extension of redemption periods, the limiting of the deficiency judgment, and restrictions on the lending power of financial institutions, have continued to exemplify governmental policy after the immediate occasion for them had passed. Except where the original enactment has carried a definite expiration date, positive action to eliminate it has rarely been taken. Successive crises, therefore, have produced an accumulation of interventionary measures; and the attitude has generally been to continue a measure, once it has become familiar or in respect to which special interests have developed.

Beginning with the crisis in farm credit about the time of World War I, and continuing through the 1930's and 1940's, crises became the occasion not only for temporary supporting and protective measures but for a number of designedly permanent new governmental operations (from the Farm Loan Board to the Farmers' Home Administration and from the Federal Housing Administration to the Public Housing Administration). Even here, the ultimate scope of these new activities was rarely contemplated at their inception. In nearly every case, however, there has been a drift that has placed steadily more responsibility and directive power in the hands of government. Despite the extensive advances resulting from the state and federal legislation of 1949, there is still no indication of the extent to which governmental control will finally impinge upon or supersede the operation of market forces.

The final source of unresolved conflict lies in the diversity of the objectives that government attempts to pursue. Thus, during the period immediately after World War II, the immediate demand was for an increased number of new houses and for the easy credit, subsidies, or grants that might be helpful in getting them built quickly and in enabling families to acquire them when built. Yet longer range considerations required that demand be held back as much as possible while the risk of inflation was present, an objective that called for measures contrary to those invoked for the first purpose. Where long range objectives conflict with shorter run demands, political pressures are almost certain to tip the balance to the latter.

But even among concurrent purposes, conflicts in governmental policies are frequent. The purposes of the housing agencies, for example, have often been at variance with those of the supervisory agencies. The desire to encourage equity investment in income-producing property has been countered by the tax policy.

The problems raised by these unresolved conflicts in public policy are of immediate and inescapable concern to all participants

in realty finance whether as lenders or borrowers, or as private
persons, institutions, or government agencies. So far, there has been
little reason to believe that a means for bringing consistency into
the vast range of governmental impacts on real estate finance is
likely to be brought about in the near future.

Index

161

162

PUBLICATIONS OF THE
NATIONAL BUREAU OF ECONOMIC RESEARCH

GENERAL SERIES

*1. Income in the United States, its Amount and Distribution, 1909–1919 (1921)
   Wesley C. Mitchell, W. I. King, F. R. Macaulay, and O. W. Knauth 168 pp.
*2. Income in the United States, its Amount and Distribution, 1909–1919 (1922)
   Wesley C. Mitchell, W. I. King, F. R. Macaulay, and O. W. Knauth 454 pp.
*3. Distribution of Income by States in 1919 (1922)
   O. W. Knauth   36 pp.
*4. Business Cycles and Unemployment (1923)
   Committee on Unemployment and Business Cycles of the President's Conference on Unemployment, and a Special Staff of the National Bureau

                                                                        414 pp.
*5. Employment, Hours and Earnings in Prosperity and Depression, United States, 1920–1922 (1923)
   W. I. King   150 pp.
*6. The Growth of American Trade Unions, 1880–1923 (1924)
   Leo Wolman   170 pp.
 7. Income in the Various States: Its Sources and Distribution, 1919, 1920, and 1921 (1925)
   Maurice Leven   306 pp., $3.50
*8. Business Annals (1926)
   W. L. Thorp, with an introductory chapter, *Business Cycles as Revealed by Business Annals*, by *Wesley C. Mitchell*   380 pp.
 9. Migration and Business Cycles (1926)
   Harry Jerome   258 pp., $2.50
10. Business Cycles: The Problem and its Setting (1927)
   Wesley C. Mitchell   514 pp., $5.00
*11. The Behavior of Prices (1927)
   F. C. Mills   598 pp.
12. Trends in Philanthropy (1928)
   W. I. King   78 pp., $1.00
*13. Recent Economic Changes in the United States (1929)
   Committee on Unemployment and Business Cycles of the President's Conference on Unemployment, and a Special Staff of the National Bureau

                                                                 2 vols., 990 pp.
*14. International Migrations (Statistics), I (1929)
   Imre Ferenczi   1112 pp.
*15. The National Income and its Purchasing Power (1930)
   W. I. King   394 pp.
*16. Corporation Contributions to Organized Community Welfare Services (1930)
   Pierce Williams and *F. E. Croxton*   348 pp.
*17. Planning and Control of Public Works (1930)
   Leo Wolman   292 pp.
*18. International Migrations (Interpretations), II (1931)
   Ed. by *W. F. Willcox*   716 pp.

* Out of print.

165

*19. The Smoothing of Time Series (1931)
F. R. Macaulay   174 pp.

20. The Purchase of Medical Care through Fixed Periodic Payment (1932)
Pierce Williams   326 pp., $3.00

*21. Economic Tendencies in the United States (1932)
F. C. Mills   660 pp.

22. Seasonal Variations in Industry and Trade (1933)
Simon Kuznets   480 pp., $4.00

23. Production Trends in the United States Since 1870 (1934)
A. F. Burns   396 pp., $3.50

24. Strategic Factors in Business Cycles (1934)
J. M. Clark   256 pp., $1.50

25. German Business Cycles, 1924–1933 (1934)
C. T. Schmidt   308 pp., $2.50

26. Industrial Profits in the United States (1934)
R. C. Epstein   692 pp., $5.00

27. Mechanization in Industry (1934)
Harry Jerome   518 pp., $3.50

28. Corporate Profits as Shown by Audit Reports (1935)
W. A. Paton   166 pp., $1.25

29. Public Works in Prosperity and Depression (1935)
A. D. Gayer   482 pp., $3.00

30. Ebb and Flow in Trade Unionism (1936)
Leo Wolman   272 pp., $2.50

31. Prices in Recession and Recovery (1936)
Frederick C. Mills   596 pp., $4.00

*32. National Income and Capital Formation, 1919–1935 (1937)
Simon Kuznets   98 pp.

33. Some Theoretical Problems Suggested by the Movements of Interest Rates,
Bond Yields and Stock Prices in the United States Since 1856 (1938)
F. R. Macaulay   612 pp., $5.00

*34. Commodity Flow and Capital Formation, Volume I (1938)
Simon Kuznets   518 pp.

*35. Capital Consumption and Adjustment (1938)
Solomon Fabricant   291 pp.

*36. The Structure of Manufacturing Production, A Cross-Section View (1939)
C. A. Bliss   248 pp.

*37. The International Gold Standard Reinterpreted, 1914–1934 (1940)
William Adams Brown, Jr.   2 vols., 1474 pp.

38. Residential Real Estate, Its Economic Position as Shown by Values, Rents,
Family Incomes, Financing, and Construction, together with Estimates for
All Real Estate (1941)
D. L. Wickens   330 pp., $3.50

*39. The Output of Manufacturing Industries, 1899–1937 (1940)
Solomon Fabricant   710 pp.

40. National Income and its Composition, 1919–1938 (1941)
Simon Kuznets   956 pp., $5.00

* Out of print.

*41. Employment in Manufacturing, 1899–1939: An Analysis of its Relation to the Volume of Production (1942)
Solomon Fabricant   382 pp.

*42. American Agriculture, 1899–1939: A Study of Output, Employment and Productivity (1942)
Harold Barger and *H. H. Landsberg*   462 pp.

*43. The Mining Industries, 1899–1939: A Study of Output, Employment and Productivity (1944)
Harold Barger and *H. H. Landsberg*   462 pp.

44. National Product in Wartime (1945)
Simon Kuznets   174 pp., $2.00

*45. Income from Independent Professional Practice (1945)
Milton Friedman and *Simon Kuznets*   636 pp.

46. National Product Since 1869 (1946)
Simon Kuznets   256 pp., $3.00

47. Output and Productivity in the Electric and Gas Utilities, 1899–1942 (1946)
J. M. Gould   208 pp., $3.00

48. Value of Commodity Output Since 1869 (1947)
W. H. Shaw   320 pp., $4.00

49. Business Incorporations in the United States, 1800–1943 (1948)
G. Heberton Evans, Jr.   192 pp. (8½x11), $6.00

50. The Statistical Agencies of the Federal Government: A Report to the Commission on Organization of the Executive Branch of the Government (1949)
F. C. Mills and *C. D. Long*   224 pp., $2.00

STUDIES IN BUSINESS CYCLES

1. The Problem and its Setting (1927)
Wesley C. Mitchell   514 pp., $5.00

2. Measuring Business Cycles (1946)
A. F. Burns and *Wesley C. Mitchell*   592 pp., $5.00

3. American Transportation in Prosperity and Depression (1948)
Thor Hultgren   432 pp., $5.00

TWENTY-FIFTH ANNIVERSARY SERIES

1. National Income: A Summary of Findings (1946)
Simon Kuznets   160 pp., $1.50

*2. Price-Quantity Interactions in Business Cycles (1946)
Frederick C. Mills   158 pp.

3. Economic Research and the Development of Economic Science and Public Policy (1946)
Twelve Papers Presented at the Twenty-fifth Anniversary Meeting of the National Bureau of Economic Research   208 pp., $1.00

4. Trends in Output and Employment (1947)
George J. Stigler   80 pp., $1.00

CONFERENCE ON RESEARCH IN INCOME AND WEALTH
STUDIES IN INCOME AND WEALTH

1. (1937)   370 pp., $2.50
*2. (1938)   358 pp.

* Out of print.

*3. (1939)   508 pp.
*4. Outlay and Income in the United States, 1921–1938 (1942)
    Harold Barger   420 pp.
*5. Income Size Distributions in the United States, Part I (1943)   160 pp.
*6. (1944)   302 pp.
*7. Changes in Income Distribution During the Great Depression (1946)
    Horst Mendershausen   192 pp.
*8. (1946)   311 pp.
 9. Analysis of Wisconsin Income (1948)
    F. A. Hanna, J. A. Pechman, S. M. Lerner   261 pp., $3.50
10. 1947
    Eight papers on proposed changes in the measurement of national income
    and product by the Department of Commerce; problems of international
    comparisons of income and wealth; the nation's 'economic budget' and fore-
    casting gross national product and employment during the transition period;
    and savings, income distribution, and resource distribution patterns.
                                                          352 pp., $4.50
11. (1949)
    Six papers on the industrial distribution of manpower, real incomes in dis-
    similar geographic areas, national income forecasting, and the saving-income
    ratio.   464 pp., $6.00
12. (1950)
    Thirteen papers on national wealth.   608 pp., $6.00

CONFERENCE ON PRICE RESEARCH
 *1. Report of the Committee on Prices in the Bituminous Coal Industry (1938)
                                                                     168 pp.
 *2. Textile Markets—Their Structure in Relation to Price Research (1939)
                                                                     290 pp.
 *3. Price Research in the Steel and Petroleum Industries (1939)   188 pp.
  4. Cost Behavior and Price Policy (1943)
     By the Committee on Price Determination   376 pp., $3.00

FISCAL STUDIES
 *1. Fiscal Planning for Total War (1942)
     W. L. Crum, J. F. Fennelly, and L. H. Seltzer   388 pp.
  2. Taxable and Business Income (1949)
     Dan T. Smith and J. Keith Butters   368 pp., $4.00

FINANCIAL RESEARCH PROGRAM
  I A PROGRAM OF FINANCIAL RESEARCH
    One: Report of the Exploratory Committee on Financial
    Research (1937)   96 pp., $1.00
    Two: Inventory of Current Research on Financial Problems
    (1937)   264 pp., $1.50
 II STUDIES IN CONSUMER INSTALMENT FINANCING
 *1. Personal Finance Companies and Their Credit Practices (1940)
     R. A. Young and Associates   192 pp.

* Out of print.

* Out of print.

170 PUBLICATIONS

OCCASIONAL PAPERS

*1. Manufacturing Output, 1929–1937 (December 1940)
   Solomon Fabricant
*2. National Income, 1919–1938 (April 1941)
   Simon Kuznets
 3. Finished Commodities Since 1879, Output and its Composition (August 1941)
   William H. Shaw $.25
*4. The Relation Between Factory Employment and Output Since 1899
   (December 1941)
   Solomon Fabricant
 5. Railway Freight Traffic in Prosperity and Depression (February 1942)
   Thor Hultgren $.25
*6. Uses of National Income in Peace and War (March 1942)
   Simon Kuznets
*7. Productivity of Labor in Peace and War (September 1942)
   Solomon Fabricant
*8. The Banking System and War Finance (February 1943)
   Charles R. Whittlesey
*9. Wartime 'Prosperity' and the Future (March 1943)
   Wesley C. Mitchell
10. The Effect of War on Business Financing: Manufacturing and
   Trade, World War I (November 1943)
   C. H. Schmidt and *R. A. Young* $.50
11. The Effect of War on Currency and Deposits (September 1943)
   Charles R. Whittlesey $.35
12. Prices in a War Economy: Some Aspects of the Present Price
   Structure of the United States (October 1943)
   Frederick C. Mills $.50
13. Railroad Travel and the State of Business (December 1943)
   Thor Hultgren $.35
14. The Labor Force in Wartime America (March 1944)
   Clarence D. Long $.50
15. Railway Traffic Expansion and Use of Resources in World
   War II (February 1944)
   Thor Hultgren $.35
16. British and American Plans for International Currency
   Stabilization (December 1943)
   J. H. Riddle $.35
17. National Product, War and Prewar (February 1944)
   Simon Kuznets $.50
18. Production of Industrial Materials in World Wars I
   and II (March 1944)
   Geoffrey H. Moore $.50
19. Canada's Financial System in War (April 1944)
   Benjamin H. Higgins $.50
20. Nazi War Finance and Banking (April 1944)
   Otto Nathan $.50
*21. The Federal Reserve System in Wartime (January 1945)
   Anna Youngman

   * Out of print.

22. Bank Liquidity and the War (May 1945)
    Charles R. Whittlesey $.50
23. Labor Savings in American Industry, 1899–1939 (Nov. 1945)
    Solomon Fabricant $.50
24. Domestic Servants in the United States, 1900–1940 (April 1946)
    George J. Stigler $.50
25. Recent Developments in Dominion-Provincial Fiscal Relations
    in Canada (March 1948)
    J. A. Maxwell $.50
26. The Role of Inventories in Business Cycles (May 1948)
    Moses Abramovitz $.50
27. The Structure of Postwar Prices (July 1948)
    Frederick C. Mills $.75
28. Lombard Street in War and Reconstruction (June 1949)
    Benjamin H. Higgins $1.00
29. The Rising Trend of Government Employment (June 1949)
    Solomon Fabricant $.50
30. Costs and Returns on Farm Mortgage Lending by Life
    Insurance Companies, 1945–1947 (August 1949)
    R. J. Saulnier $1.00
31. Statistical Indicators of Cyclical Revivals and Recessions
    (April 1950)
    Geoffrey H. Moore $1.50
32. Cyclical Diversities in the Fortunes of Industrial Corporations
    (May 1950)
    Thor Hultgren $.50
33. Employment and Compensation in Education (May 1950)
    George J. Stigler $1.00

TECHNICAL PAPERS

*1. A Significance Test for Time Series and Other Ordered
    Observations (September 1941)
    W. Allen Wallis and *Geoffrey H. Moore*
*2. The Relation of Cost to Output for a Leather Belt Shop
    (December 1941)
    *Joel Dean, with a Memorandum on Certain Problems in the
    Empirical Study of Costs by C. Reinold Noyes*
 3. Basic Yields of Corporate Bonds, 1900–1942 (June 1942)
    David Durand $.50
 4. Currency Held by the Public, the Banks, and the Treasury,
    Monthly, December 1917–December 1944 (January 1947)
    Anna Jacobson Schwartz and *Elma Oliver* $.75
 5. Concerning a New Federal Financial Statement (December 1947)
    Morris A. Copeland $1.00
*6. Basic Yields of Bonds, 1926–1947: Their Measurement and
    Pattern (December 1947)
    David Durand and *Willis J. Winn*

* Out of print.

NATIONAL BUREAU OF ECONOMIC RESEARCH

1819 Broadway, New York 23, N. Y.

Date Due